The World's
Craziest Cats
& other stories

D1638256

© Chris Pascoe
Illustrations by Amanda Dixon
Published in Great Britain by D C Thomson & Co. Ltd.,
185 Fleet Street, London EC4A 2HS.
www.dcthomson.co.uk

The World's Craziest Cats & other stories

Welcome to the second collection
of Chris Pascoe's My Weekly columns.
In the course of his day job as a professional
cat sitter, Chris comes across cats of all kinds
– brave, timid, feisty and affectionate. But they
all have foibles of one sort or another, some
more antisocial than others, and there's
one thing Chris can guarantee –
he never has a dull day!

CONTENTS

The World's Craziest Cats

Chris Pascoe Collection 2

Every Day's A Disaster

About The Author

Fancy That

IN A FLAP!

How many ways are there to get through a catflap? Chris is still counting

I saac Newton is remembered for his scientific genius, but while most people automatically connect him with falling apples and gravity, many are unaware that he also invented the catflap – albeit in an absent-minded sort of way.

Newton's cat had a habit of constantly interrupting his complicated calculations by demanding to be let out, so while pondering such matters as the weight of Planet Earth, Isaac whipped up a small swinging door within his own door, elevating himself to Hero of the Feline Race.

Of course, some cats have more trouble negotiating catflaps than others. I've seen a great many catflap-related incidents during my years spent working for cats.

He skated across the floor, the frame still around his neck

A huge ginger Tom hammered through his flap so hard and fast that he ended up skating across the kitchen floor with the frame of the catflap still wrapped around his neck. A petite Tortie named Nora can't seem to go through a catflap without getting stuck halfway, all four legs off the ground and rocking gently on her belly until rescued. Roger, a cross-eyed black and white, doesn't go through his catflap but instead likes to lick it. On more than one occasion this behaviour has ended with him trapping his tongue between flap and frame.

9

My own cat Brum had many problems with catflaps. Over the months his attempts to employ it as a legitimate door progressed from an early 100% failure rate through many experimental (mainly doomed) approach angles, to total disaster. He even tried climbing through backwards, which presented the disturbing spectacle of a tabby rear-end suddenly appearing from nowhere, wiggling at you for ten minutes, then just as suddenly disappearing.

He eventually developed a technique in total contrast to his normal nervy one-paw-at-a-time bunch-up – launching himself headfirst at the flap. This only almost worked. Speaking in an aerodynamic sense, something was always horribly wrong with Brum. He consistently executed magnificent back-flips on the way – he'd hit the flap all four paws pointing down but by the time he was through, they'd all be pointing to the sky.

His worst moment came when there was no catflap at all. We'd had new doors installed, you see, and hadn't yet re-installed Brum's flap. How he failed to notice there was no longer a hole in the door, I'll never know.

Still employing his newly adopted, no-compromise approach to catflapping, he came charging across the patio and launched himself headfirst into a solid wood door, hitting it so hard that his rear legs shot way up over his head. After a stunned moment, he began nonchalantly washing, as cats do when highly embarrassed, as if to suggest that this was not in any way an accident.

So on reflection you have a lot to answer for, Mr Isaac Newton, with your dangerous little swinging doors. I think a number of pointy-eared furry friends of mine would like a quiet word.

HOPPING MAD

The confrontation was odd enough – but what followed was just weird...

I mentioned my cat Brum in the last story, in connection with Isaac Newton. An unlikely duo to be mentioned in the same sentence I admit, especially as Brum, while being the loveliest long- haired tabby you could ever meet, wasn't much brighter than my rabbit.

In short, he was a walking disaster area. How many cats do you know who've set their own head on fire, fallen 20 feet onto a moving car, blown up the household electrics, lost a year-long war with a sparrow and become romantically entangled with a washing machine?

One warm sunny day in my back garden, I think I discovered Brum's intellectual double.

From nowhere, a frog hopped onto the lawn just as Brum emerged from under a bush, as usual covered in so much of the said bush that he looked as if he was camouflaged and on a Commando mission.

An edgy frog regarded a scruffy tabby. A battle was underway

Brum stopped dead in his tracks and stared at the frog. The frog stopped hopping and stared at Brum. A profound psychological battle was underway.

Suddenly, the frog jumped a foot in the air and landed back on exactly the same spot. Brum looked astonished and then,

unexpectedly, he too jumped a foot in the air, all four legs leaving the ground at once, and landed where he'd taken off.

An edgy frog regarded a scruffy tabby. The frog leapt into the air. The moment he landed, Brum shot into the air. Brum landed, the frog jumped. The frog landed, Brum jumped. The frog jumped again, Brum jumped again. It was one of the most ridiculous sights I've ever seen, and thanks to Ted and Brum, I've seen a few. It was as if I were watching a cat and a frog on an invisible see-saw.

The frog stared long and hard at Brum, decided this encounter was going nowhere, and hopped off into the distance, leaving a clearly perplexed tabby cat alone on the lawn. He stared long and hard at the space recently vacated by the frog, and then long and hard at me.

"Yes!" I said. "You won a jump-off with a frog. Well done, Brum."

Brum seemed happy with this comment (cats don't really get sarcasm) and jumped up onto my lap, covering me in sticky-burrs and garden foliage. After a few minutes ecstatic purring in celebration of his victory, he jumped down, ran the length of the lawn and leapt straight into the fish pond. I have no idea why. It wasn't something he usually did.

As I watched a soaked, bedraggled and extremely angry-looking tabby scramble up the bank and collapse sideways onto the lawn, I pondered the unlikely event I'd just witnessed.

Had it been purely down to Brum's incredibly poor sense of co-ordination or…? Brum had behaved like a frog for five minutes and then jumped in a pond.

I decided there was mind control at work here, and that the frog obviously had a level of intellectual ability that neither Brum or I could ever hope to comprehend.

Did I just say I was less intelligent than a frog?

CATS EYES

Phobias are strange things… but what if the fear is entirely justified?

I once read quite an alarming fact on My Weekly's Fancy That! page. I was lounging happily on my sofa, submerged in a couple of slightly unhinged cats (Bodmin, my semi-feral panther-like giant, and Jojo, my haughty-tortie) when I came across a fact about a little-known phobia named anatidaephobia.

Anatidaephobia is the fear that somewhere, somehow, a duck is watching you.

A duck is watching you? What? I sat pondering this for a moment until a big wet sloppy face rub from Jojo brought me to my senses, but I couldn't help but wonder if a similar phobia existed with regard to cats. Because, I thought, if the phobia exists, it would explain a few things about my father.

When he closed his eyes the room was empty, the door locked

You see, Dad spent many years totally convinced that my childhood cat Cindy was watching his every move. Cindy was jet-black with four white paws and a white chin. She looked like Batman – Batman in white ankle socks. Cindy was scheming, clever, vicious and deadly. We liked her a lot. But Dad wasn't so keen, claiming that no matter where he was, no matter what he was doing, he could sense her presence, and that he knew, absolutely knew, that she was staring at him.

Now, my father may never have been the sharpest tool in the

15

box, a characteristic he's proudly passed down to me, but he did have a point.

While sitting at the dinner table, Dad would constantly glance out through the patio doors, looking for signs of Cindy. We'd all laugh at his paranoia but then, very often, we'd spot a small black and white face in the bushes… staring straight at Dad.

Once, he was relaxing in the bath, eyes shut, music on, singing and humming. He opened his eyes to grab the shampoo… and almost had a heart attack. There, sitting on the toilet cistern and beaming happily at him, was Cindy.

When he'd closed his eyes the room had been empty, the door locked. At this point, he must truly have believed that Cindy was living up to that old black-cat reputation, and that a broomstick was parked nearby.

A little detective work, however, revealed how she'd performed this piece of magic. A bedroom's net curtains were hanging out through the window fanlight. She'd obviously climbed out of the bedroom window, walked along the roof and squeezed in through the bathroom fanlight.

The question is, why? Seeing my father in the bath was something most people surely would have wanted to avoid, but Cindy actually risked life and paw just to be there, on that cistern, when he opened his eyes.

I've just answered my own questions, haven't I? He didn't have a phobia at all. A cat really was watching his every move. Why did she do it? Because all cats are mad. Problem solved.

There doesn't seem to be a feline version of the marvellous anatidaephobia. But ailurophobia is one I won't want to be developing (irrational fear of cats). That wouldn't bode well for Jojo and Bodmin at all! 🐾

ALL AT SEA!

Chris has a theory about the identity of Brighton's seafaring moggy

I have recently returned from a week's holiday, courtesy of a very good ex-customer who moved to Brighton and offered us the opportunity to continue looking after her Burmese cat, Olive, in exchange for free accommodation. A freeloading busman's holiday!

It was a nice, relaxing week, with Olive acting the perfect hostess. Well… only if the standard perfect hostess greets you by vomiting on your shoes then skulking off to bed and pointedly ignoring you for three days.

Sam now thought explosions were simply part of life

The most unusual moment of the week came on Brighton pier. I was sitting on a courtesy deckchair trying to read a newspaper in the howling wind when a small boat sailed towards the pier. As it drew level, I started in surprise – staring straight at me from the deck was a large ginger cat. Do cats (and the odd rabbit) hunt me down wherever I go – even when I'm 100 metres out in the English Channel?

The ginger cat and I stared at one another, both resisting the urge to wave, until he disappeared around the end of the pier. The most astounding thing was that I didn't see anyone else on the boat. I'm hoping somebody was in the small cabin at the front, but I couldn't see them. I found myself wondering if I should perhaps have been looking for an owl instead. The boat wasn't pea-green though, or particularly beautiful.

The whole thing brought to mind a feline hero of mine named Unsinkable Sam. Unsinkable Sam was a World War II ship's cat, originally with the German Navy, and a floating furball of bad luck. The fact that Sam's first naval posting was with one of the world's most famously ill-fated battleships, The Bismarck, says it all. The Bismarck was quickly torpedoed to the bottom of the sea, but a frantically catty-paddling Unsinkable was hauled aboard Britain's HMS Cossack.

With Sam aboard, the Cossack sailed on before being torpedoed by a U-Boat. A seriously fed-up and drenched Unsinkable once again found himself being dragged from the ocean, this time onto HMS Ark Royal. The crew of the Ark Royal were now in serious trouble – Unsinkable Sam was aboard. They didn't stand a chance, and were duly blown up. Unsinkable, by now no doubt thinking that massive explosions followed by 100mph splashdowns in the Atlantic Ocean were just part of everyday life, swam over to the nearest ship and waited for a sailor from HMS Legion to rescue him.

Sam, though, had now become a very infamous cat indeed. When the crew of HMS Legion realised with horror just what they'd pulled out of the sea, it was to their great credit that they didn't throw him back. Instead they sailed carefully and nervously back to England, and put him ashore. Greatly relieved, they sailed happily away and were sunk by a Stuka bomber.

As for Unsinkable Sam, I've scoured history and can find no further trace of him. Unless – hmmm, I wonder… just who exactly was that mysterious ginger tom who sailed past Brighton Pier? 🐾

ON THE CATWALK

A cat lead is no embarrassment to the cat... but it's mortifying for the walker

I've recently been looking after a cat named Rollo. He's a one-eyed ginger tom rogue and one of my favourites.

Rollo is one of those that could safely be referred to as a bit unlucky on the health front. He only has one working eye, he's half-deaf and has a thyroid condition requiring tablets exactly 12 hours apart. His owner has warned that, if I miss a tablet, his remaining eye could "explode". No pressure then.

Rollo's reduced senses obviously make him a bit of a liability when out on his own. In fact, he's all over the place. Walking up to a growling Rottweiler on the common near his home and tentatively sniffing its front paws was a deciding factor in his owner's decision to allow him out only on a cat-lead.

He will occasionally trip over my feet or walk straight into a tree

Having to take a cat out for a walk on a lead means of course that I face regular humiliation. Once every 12 hours, in fact. On a patch of common land mainly frequented by large macho dog owners with large macho dogs, I can regularly be seen flouncing around with a small ginger cat on a lead.

It doesn't help that the said cat will occasionally trip over my

feet or walk straight into a tree.

But, half-blind, half-deaf, on constant medication, Rollo is still an extremely happy, friendly and confident cat. As long as he's got his food, his treats and me to drag around a field, all's well with his little world.

Actually, Rollo isn't the first cat I've taken walkies.

A number of years ago, I briefly moved into a converted farm building with my own cat Brum, the hero (or possibly anti-hero) of my first book. The farm lay beside a busy main road so I decided using a cat-lead would be a good way of carefully introducing him to his new surroundings.

On our first trip out, Brum suddenly jumped onto the top of an eight-foot-high oil container, wrenching my arm abruptly over my head. Knowing that the top of the container was rusty, my immediate concern was that Brum could fall through into the oil (this being the sort of thing Brum normally did) and so I didn't dare let go of the lead. And this, sadly, was how the local farmer and his son found me – my arm stretched into the sky and a cat-lead disappearing over the edge of an oil drum.

A dry humoured, mickey-taking man at the best of times, the farmer couldn't resist completely ignoring my dilemma and happily talking to me about the weather for five minutes. Eventually, after what seemed an arm-aching eternity, his face darkened, he looked me straight in the eye and whispered conspiratorially, "You do know you got a cat on a bit o'string there, do you lad?"

I think I answered with something inane like "Eh, oh, yes I do, thank you," but the mind sometimes mercifully manages to block out our most embarrassing moments.

Which probably explains why I can't remember much of my life at all.

SUSPICIOUS MIND

Benny the cat was easy to please… but his owner's phone calls caused panic!

My all time craziest cat-sitting client has just emigrated to the other side of the planet. On the one hand this is sad because I'll miss her wonderful and equally crazy cat Benny. On the other hand, it's great because I can now talk about her without her knowing. There are so many things I've been burning to tell you about, I don't know where to start, so I'll go alphabetical and start with A for Ants.

After my very first booking with Benny I told him I hoped his owner Jennifer would be happy with the service and book me to visit again. However, the next morning Jennifer rang me.

"Hi Chris. Thanks for looking after Benny – he was very content when I got home. There's just one thing I need to ask though… did you put ants in my kitchen?"

Not did I see ants in the kitchen – did I actually put them there. I envisaged painstakingly plucking ants from the garden and walking them into the house, and then dismissed the image. Even I wouldn't do that.

"Do you mean did I see any?" I replied carefully, "I saw one near the oven, but…"

"So you're saying you didn't put them there?"

"Put them there? No, why would I…"

"OK, Chris, say no more. You said you didn't do it and that's good enough for me."

Two bookings later, after I'd had a nice time looking after Benny in his warm house during a rain-soaked week, I got yet another call from Jennifer.

"Chris – I've just got home and I'm not at all happy!"

"Oh no!" I blurted out, panicking. "Is Benny OK?"

"Benny's fine. Did you cut my apple tree down?"

"Your apple tree? No, I didn't even know you had an apple tr–"

"Are you sure?"

I was sure. I'd definitely know if I'd chopped a tree down. Also, the fact that I hadn't been in Jennifer's garden – not even to collect kitchen ants – meant I was absolutely certain.

Two months later she booked me again. Apparently her neighbour had removed the apple tree, mainly on account of it being his tree and in his garden. Jennifer missed the overhanging branches terribly though. I reluctantly accepted the booking, even though I was now slightly frightened.

Things settled down for a few bookings, but I always made sure to count the trees on first and last visits. It wasn't over though…

I'm sure I would remember chopping down an apple tree…

Ring-ring went the phone the morning after a Jennifer booking. My heart sank and, slightly trembling, I answered the phone.

"Chris? I'm sorry to have to ask, but were you sick in the back bedroom?"

Ants, apples and accidents – Benny's accident not mine, but Jennifer insisted it wasn't "at all like cat sick" – and I haven't got past the letter A. I have to say things got much better with Jennifer after that and we became firm friends but I'm pretty sure she still thinks I ate her begonias… 🐾

OOH LA LA!

Chris – unsuccessfully – ponders the world of cats in several languages

Well, I heard a great story the other day. It was about a Chinese lady with little English who, on discovering a mouse in her hotel room, immediately phoned down to reception.

When reception answered, she suddenly realised she had no idea of the English word for mouse, or how to report the situation. What she then said was one of the most charmingly wonderful things I've ever heard…

"Hello. Tom & Jerry? Jerry's here."

I love that!

Nevertheless, it puts me in mind of a wholly less charming piece of translation in a French hotel we once visited with my parents.

Having crossed the channel on a special offer ferry ticket (full price, but with a free bottle of any wine we don't like) we checked into our hotel. It was a note on the hotel-restaurant door that caught my eye:

Dinner guests please to note – if you have any strange dietary requirements, please expose yourself to restaurant staff.

I don't have any strange dietary requirements, but my Dad does. We decided to eat in town that night.

Dad has had a few translation problems of his own in the past, most notably on the first night of his honeymoon. Attempting to impress Mum but failing miserably (he certainly started as he meant to carry on) he attempted to order desserts in Spanish.

Five minutes later he was served a gigantic bowl of vinegar. He can't remember what it was he actually tried to order,

but knowing him as I do, it was probably… a gigantic bowl of vinegar!

Not that I have any room to comment. On another French trip – on this occasion house-sitting for a friend while looking after her umpteen cats – a French woman came to my door one day (they have a lot of French women in France). We were unable to understand each another, but the fact she kept repeating the word "chat" and pointing at the road soon had me alarmed and carrying out a feline head count. All were present – except one, named Lottie.

I frantically searched the house – no sign. Just as my heart began to sink, I finally spotted her.

Another much larger cat had settled in his bed, not worrying at all that Lottie was already in it. Only a worried pointy-eared face

The French cat settled down, oblivious to Lottie beneath

protruded from beneath his giant furry midriff.

Relieved, I returned to my visitor, who'd been waiting patiently at the door. As our conversation continued, my attempts at French led her to firmly believe I was German.

Finally I grabbed my laptop, and through Google-Translate, we were able to establish that she lived next door, and couldn't find her ginger and white cat.

I later found out that the literal French translation of my typed response must have made me look rather odd: I have not seen a cat of these colours. If I see one, I will tell him about you.

She shook her head and left. I found her cat in the lounge an hour later. It bit me. 🐾

SPARROW HOOKED

In a war between bird and cat there's usually a feline victor – but not for this pussy

Now that my book, You Can Take the Cat out of Slough, has been re-released in paperback, I've found myself talking repeatedly about the book's hapless feline hero Brum. There's always a lot to talk about when it comes to Brum, a cat who's created enough mayhem to fill two books. Brum's blown up the household electrics, set fire to his own head, fallen 20 feet onto a moving car… and that's just for starters.

I doubt he intended to cause damage, but damage was done

A typical Brum "achievement" can be summed up by his ill-fated war with a sparrow. Most cats would be confident of quick victory… in under 15 seconds. Not Brum. Not only did the war drag on for a month, Brum lost. True, the sparrow had air superiority, but on the ground, claw-to-paw, Brum should have at least held his own.

How the war started is unknown, but Brum certainly had a penchant for climbing trees. My assumption would be that on one of his climbing expeditions, he came across the sparrow's nest. I doubt that he'd have intended to cause damage, but damage would almost certainly have been done.

You see, Brum's climbing technique is desperately clawing at every single leaf and twig as he attempted not to fall… then falling. I have a mental picture of Brum frantically tearing the nest to pieces as a livid sparrow stared in disbelief.

That's just conjecture, but what is a "known-known" as Donald Rumsfeld* once said (*please look the video up!) is that this sparrow took a violent dislike to Brum.

I first became aware Brum was having bird problems when I spotted him scramble over the lip of next-door's fence, wide-eyed and dishevelled and swiping at thin air. At first I thought he was trying out a new dance routine, but then came the sparrow. A peck and a hit, a swipe and a miss, again and again until Brum half fell from the fence and ran for cover. The sparrow looked astonished. Normally Brum's speed and agility more closely resembled that of a house brick than a streamlined feline killing-machine.

From then on, wherever Brum let his defences down, the sparrow found him, and his defences weren't great. Getting close to a wall for protection was a smart move by Brum… sitting staring at it while the sparrow pecked the back of his ears wasn't.

It ended where it began; on my neighbour's fence. Caught in the open, Brum sat swiping at the sparrow like a sedated King Kong and, like King Kong, he eventually plummeted. Unlike King Kong, he fell straight through my neighbour's plastic green house roof.

A delighted sparrow, a wrecked greenhouse and a repair bill. Just a normal Brum day, really. 🐾

LITTER LOUT!

Chris gallantly takes the blame for his charges – and unnerves a neighbour

I f you're a regular reader of my columns in My Weekly you'll maybe remember my dead rodent episode in Tesco.

You probably won't be at all surprised to hear that this wasn't my first embarrassing incident caused by the careless transportation of cat detritus. The first, and worst, was quite a while ago, while visiting a salubrious apartment block on a posh estate in a very posh village.

I was looking after a pair of cats named Herman and Morticia; a roguish ginger boy and his tortoiseshell flatmate. Herman's two great pleasures in life are eating everything in sight and killing everything that moves.

Haughty Morticia treats anything Herman does with total disdain

Strangely though, he doesn't combine the two hobbies – never eating his prey. Morticia, being a classic haughty-tortie, treats everything Herman does with total disdain, so there was no way she'd be eating any of it either. Consequently, I'd generally walk into their apartment to find various ex-wildlife.

One pursuit Herman and Morticia do share, though, is the filling of their litter tray to bursting point on a daily basis, despite having a catflap and being able to use neighbour's flower beds, as most polite cats do.

Anyway, after spending some quality time with this scarily

named pair, I picked up my binbag of horror containing a dead rat and the day's foul litter tray offerings and headed for the outdoor bins. As I reached the communal corridor front door, I put my bag down to lift the latch. It was at this point that the bag split. It wasn't a big split, but onto the doormat rolled a very large piece of poo (Herman's, of course – I don't want to embarrass Morticia here). OK, I thought. Get the damaged bag to the bins as fast as possible, then come back and clear up the mess.

I pinched the split and ran through the door, losing a little more of the contents along the way, including the rat just outside, but reached the bins and disposed of the bag with minimum spillage – so far damage-limitation was good. I raced back to the hall, where I found a business-suited lady from a neighbouring apartment about to leaving the building, staring in shock at a large poo on the doormat. Not so good.

"It's OK," I said hurriedly with a smile. "That's my fault – bit of an accident a minute ago – I'm just going to get some tissues."

The look on her face darkened considerably, as mine became totally crimson as I realised exactly what I'd just said. She smiled a little nervously and stepped gingerly over the doormat and through the door.

"Oh – watch out for the rat!" I called after her.

Returning to the apartment, I found Herman climbing in through the catflap with a rat clamped between his teeth. He'd retrieved the corpse I'd just dropped, making my goodbye shout to the neighbour utterly nonsensical.

Unless, of course, she assumed Rat to be my nickname and "Watch out for the rat!" my war-cry after defecating on people's doorsteps. Either way, I didn't come out of it looking good.

Thanks, Herman.

FANCY THAT!

Cat facts to make you go "meow"

A group of cats is called a clowder.

Kittens start to dream when they're about a week old.

Kittens sleep a lot because their body releases a growth hormone only when they're asleep.

Cats can't see directly below their noses, that's why they miss food directly below them.

A genetic mutation means cats can't taste sugar.

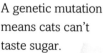

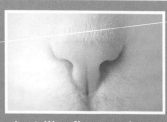

Just like fingerprints, every cat's nose pad is different.

By 1952, Dusty—a Tabby from Texas—had given birth to a total number of 420 kittens in her lifetime.

The cheetah is the world's fastest cat, and can reach speeds of 70 mph.

Isaac Newton invented the catflap after his own cat kept opening the door and ruining his experiments.

Cats have kidneys that can filter out salt meaning that, unlike humans, they can drink seawater.

Jack and Donna Wright of Ontario, Canada made their way into the Guinness World Records for having the highest number of cats, with a staggering 689 cats.

The largest known litter produced was 19 kittens in Oxfordshire in 1970.

A cat's brain is far more complex than a dog's.

Cats can make over 100 vocal sounds.

Ancient Egyptians shaved their eyebrows in mourning when their cats died and if someone killed a cat, he or she could be punished with a death penalty.

STRICTLY WALTZING

I love my cat sitting job – I really couldn't think of any better way to spend my days than visiting a succession of friendly, affectionate cats. Then I met Miranda…

Miranda is a three-year-old tabby, but looks more like a kitten. Giant eyes and a permanently startled expression add to the cute-kitten appearance.

As cute as Miranda looks, she quickly proved to be one of my deadliest adversaries.

Now, that's just plain wrong, isn't it? I should surely be caring lovingly for the cats in my charge. Pampering them, petting them, feeding them… not referring to them as adversaries? Miranda gave me little choice in the matter.

Her owners warned me she could be "feisty", but when I'd collected the keys, she'd been a gentle, purring ball of fur. Her owner cradled her in her arms, and Miranda happily pushed her face into my outstretched hand.

Feisty? I thought. Pah! That's not feisty – that's just fluffy!

When I arrived at Miranda's two days later, I bent down to say hello, stretching my hand out, expecting another affectionate nuzzle. I just didn't see that paw coming.

There was a hiss, a blur of motion, and then searing pain across my fingers. Suddenly I had a small tabby attached to me, all four sets of claws embedded in my arm while sharp teeth sank into

my hand. I couldn't think of anything useful to say, so I just said "OUCH" and sank to my knees.

The sinking to the knees bit was a little over-dramatic, I know, but I think it looked quite good. The purpose though was to get to Miranda's level rather than have her dangling in mid-air, gradually removing flesh.

After careful removal, I walked slowly to the kitchen, conscious of low, growling sounds behind me. Grabbing a tin of appeasing food, I called, "Dinner!"

A thump against the back of my leg told me Miranda wasn't prepared to accept my food offer. The claws in my calf confirmed this.

Have you ever tried to remove a cat from the back of your leg?

Ever tried to remove a cat from the back of your leg? Anybody witnessing the event would have seen a man twirling across the kitchen floor with a cat attached to his leg, like a feline/fat bloke version of Strictly.

As I stumbled into the lounge I revised my plans – dancing with Miranda would solve nothing, and it also hurt. Propping myself against the sofa I finally removed her for a second time.

Over the next few days, I employed a system involving gloves, careful eye contact, slow movement and various cunning distraction techniques. This all failed.

By day four, though, Miranda got bored of biting me. Now, after seven days, I can happily add her to my aforementioned list of likeable clients.

I won't be visiting in shorts any time soon, though.

SPINE TICKLER!

Which spirits from the other side has Chris managed to disturb?

I've mentioned before that some of my pet-sitting visits can be a bit creepy. Mainly this is because I visit empty old houses – well, empty but for the odd cat and sometimes bonus chameleon, hamster or violent rat – often on dark, dismal evenings.

I creep around these places, trying hard not to jump at every creak or bump from empty rooms above me, and attempting to ignore the wind howling mournfully down ancient chimneys and through old unlit fireplaces.

Happily, everything that's ever shaken me up in these places has been down to my own overactive imagination or the sudden jump-inducing appearance of cats at already edgy moments. Until now.

I had my first ever truly supernatural experience on a visit this week. Or at least, the first experience I've as yet found no way of explaining.

Suddenly and inexplicably, I felt extremely uneasy

It was six am and I was in a very old house in the very old village of Penn. For lovers of random trivia, Pennsylvania, USA is actually named after William Penn…from Penn.

Anyway, back to me in this house, which pre-dates the existence

of Pennsylvania or the United States. I had to give the cat residing there, Bonnie, her medication and I couldn't find her anywhere in the place's maze of darkened rooms. This was important medication – without it at regular intervals 12 hours apart, she could keel over at any moment. No pressure, then.

So, I hunted every room in the house. Just when I'd run out of ideas and started thinking about leaving the country before Bonnie's big burly owner got back from holiday and found I'd killed his cat, I finally found her standing in the kitchen – the room I'd first looked in half an hour previously. Cats…

Bonnie took her tablets without any problem whatsoever, ate her breakfast and went off upstairs. I watched her from the bottom of the staircase as she disappeared into a dark room at the end of the landing. Suddenly, inexplicably, I felt extremely uneasy. And then I heard, as clear as a bell, a man's voice shout, "Do you want a tickle?"

I jumped out of my skin. I knew for sure the house was absolutely empty – I'd just searched it three times, looking under every bed, in every open cupboard, everywhere. And I knew that the room the voice seemed to come from, the one Bonnie had walked into, didn't even have any of those things – no furniture, no beds, no cupboards, it was just an old, dark empty room.

My heart pumping 10 to the dozen, I decided I had to go up there, into that room, if only to check on Bonnie.

It was the right thing to do, the brave thing to do. I honestly did think these things as I legged it out of the front door and wheel-skidded up the drive at top speed.

But how typical of me that my first ever supernatural experience wasn't a disembodied voice booming "Begone or meet thy doooommm", or even clinking chains and a "Wooooooo" but "Do you want a tickle?"

Great.

I only hope he was talking to Bonnie and not to me…

WAR GAMES

Battle lines are well-established amid the hustle and bustle of Chez Pascoe

It occurred to me the other day that our house is like one huge battleground, with many opposing armies. Okay, the armies are all one-person armies, probably much like Liechtenstein's, but you know what I mean.

There seems to be a round-robin system of conflict in place, whereby almost everyone and every animal has at least one adversary to attack, and one to fight off.

For instance, let's start with our giant ex-stray Bodmin. He's at war with the house's other two cats. He can't seem to stop himself chasing the black & white Spooky, but is extremely wary of our haughty-tortie Jojo. Bodmin just can't work Jojo out at all; how can she possibly have the audacity to snarl, growl and paw-swipe his head when she's only a third of his size? I think this causes him to reach the mistaken conclusion that there must be something fearsome about her he hasn't factored in.

Bib and Bob swim behind a rock every time I look into their tank

Consequently, her smallness terrifies him. You could just imagine Bodmin's memoirs in years to come: Jojo was a bully who constantly berated me about my size…or despite my size, one of the two. Meanwhile, Jojo's terrified of Spooky the cat who's terrified of Bodmin. It's a perfect ménage a trois – each runs from one cat and chases the other. I can imagine a cartoon version

45

of them all running around in a little circle snapping at each other's tails.

The situation on the human front is strikingly similar. My wife Lorraine finds my shouty teenage daughter Maya extremely frightening, but in turn Maya finds Lorraine pretty frightening too, particularly around 8pm on a Sunday night when Lorraine asks about her homework. I in turn find them both scary. I'm fairly on edge around Spooky too, to be honest. While none of those three are in the slightest bit scared of me, our two goldfish most certainly are. For no apparent reason, Bib and Bob immediately swim behind a rock every time I look into their tank. I suppose my giant moon-face appearing at anybody's window would be a bit shocking, but because of this habit I now only have a vague recollection of what they even look like.

Meanwhile, in a rabbit hutch regular readers know well, a feisty female bunny named Billie regularly cuffs the ears of the world's dumbest rabbit Ted who, being Ted, doesn't even know it's happening. In fact, thinking about it, Ted's the only householder not at war, mainly because he's only vaguely aware anyone else lives in the house. So, on the basis that war is stupid, does this make Ted hyper-intelligent? Just recently, he deliberately jumped on the front of his litter tray, flipping the whole lot over his head. So no, it doesn't

Speaking of Liechtenstein, did you know it has twice in recent decades been invaded by of all countries, Switzerland… and on neither occasion did anyone in Liechtenstein notice. Though they did belatedly wonder why their forest was on fire. 🐾

PURR-FECT STUDENT

Geronimo, the college cat, flags up some interesting discoveries…

My latest feline client – a lovely long-haired ginger tom named Geronimo – lives in a student apartment with, not surprisingly, students.

Geronimo's owner is a charming girl named Becky – extremely switched-on, intelligent and chatty. Her two flatmates, however, seem to have looked up "totally unfair media student stereotypes" and then followed the blueprint religiously. Rather strangely, so does Geronimo.

Upon my introductory visit to Geronimo's student digs, Becky, introduced me to her two male flatmates – both of whom grunted without once looking away from their mobile phones. She then introduced me to Geronimo, who was sitting on a chair staring intently into the corner of the room at absolutely nothing. I gave Geronimo's long ginger coat a stroke and said a few complimentary words, to be greeted with a rasping noise very similar to the grunts I'd already received.

A few days later I found him sitting in the same pizza box

At this point, Becky had to vacate the room to answer the door, and I was left with my three new grunting friends. Total silence.

I made a cheerful comment about the weather. Two grunts, a rasping noise. Wondering what to do with my arms (as you do), I began stroking Geronimo again, who sighed, gave me an extremely annoyed sideways look, stretched, and jumped down from the chair. He made it halfway across the room before collapsing sideways onto the floor and staring at the TV, which was off.

There was a loud, despairing grunt behind me as one of the students inspected an empty pizza box. Then all was still.

A few days later, visiting Geronimo in my official capacity as his feeder and carer, I found him sitting in that same pizza box. He was staring at the wall again. I stroked him, he shrugged me off and grunted irritably.

As I sat staring at the wall with him, the thought struck me that cats are not that far removed from the student, or indeed teenage, stereotype. Cats want to be fed, pampered and run around after, while doing absolutely nothing in return. They like to sleep half the day, are more active at night and believe themselves to be far cooler than us. Cats and students are virtually the same species.

I have a theory about these likenesses, and it relates to the student staple soft drink famous for giving its drinkers "wings" and keeping them frenziedly energetic until the early hours. It contains an active ingredient named Taurine.

Where else can we find this stuff? Believe it or not… in cat food. We couldn't have chosen a more twitchy, sometimes manic creature to feed something like that to.

We wonder why cats sit on fences half the night singing their heads off. We have only ourselves to blame.

DISCOMFORT AND JOY!

Dashing to the rescue of a cat under fire, Chris resorts to underhand tactics

So it's into the Christmas period we go, and as much as I love Christmas I'm always wary of winter. Snow and ice make cat-sitting much more difficult, with all that driving between one totally unappreciative feline and the next.

Something about the snow must bring out the worst in me – I have to admit that I did something I'm not particularly proud of in the snow last year. Well, I say not particularly proud…

I'd been visiting a roguishly cool cat called Penguin, very aptly named given his black and white markings and the prevailing weather conditions. We'd had some great fun, Penguin being one of those cats that loves to pounce on piles of snow, bounding around his backyard like Tigger.

One day, reluctantly leaving Penguin safely in his nice warm home and heading back out into sub-zero temperatures, I reached my car and noticed a group of teenage lads looking up into a tree while preparing snowballs. Just as I realised what it was they were looking at, the ginger cat resting in the branches became the target of a snowball volley.

Fortunately, their aims matched their empathy towards a poor little cat who was simply minding his own business and enjoying his day. Every shot missed by a mile and Ginger Tom jumped deftly to a higher branch. The young men quickly began rolling more snow for a second attempt.

Now, I did think about getting into my car and saying nothing but this was a cat – and I'm a cat-sitter. It was my duty to become a have-a-go sitter.

"Oi!" I shouted, hoping that this would adequately explain my feelings, and also that this devastatingly intellectual piece of wordplay would make the group see the error of their ways.

The resulting five snowballs that thudded into my car as I jumped into my seat convinced me I'd overdone it. As I began to pull away through more snowballs, I saw an interesting thing. There was a huge puddle of black slush in the road, directly in front of the unheroic band of cat-baiters.

What happened next was something I'll be ashamed of forever. But not that ashamed. I drove to the end of the road, performed a U-turn and accelerated back to the scene. The deluge as I skimmed the slush-pile was so great that the group completely disappeared from sight, engulfed in a torrent of wet filth. My mirror view was of stunned faces and arms spread wide in an "I'm totally saturated" posture. I'd just thrown the ultimate snowball.

This was a cat.
It was my duty

The very last thing I saw was the happy sight of Ginger Tom taking advantage of the lull in hostilities by jumping 10 feet onto a high brick wall and scurrying away to safety.

So, not my proudest moment, but a message to all those anywhere who treat our friends the cats poorly. Don't stand near slush. I'm coming. 🐾

JEOPARDY CLAWS!

Hell hath no fury like a pet whose owner Chris has accidentally insulted…

Things couldn't have started any worse with a new client last week.

The very pleasant and charming Tricia called to arrange some short-notice cat-sitting for the weekend, full of compliments about the good things she'd heard about our service, and I responded by insulting her twice within the first two minutes of our conversation.

"OK Tricia – that's all booked. Would it be convenient to collect your key on Wednesday?"

"Um, not Wednesday. I'm having a hair, pampering and spa day. Got to make myself beautiful for the weekend!"

"That'll be hard work…"

You're thinking What? Why on earth would he say that? As, I'm sure, was Tricia.

I honestly intended a friendly, ironic quip about relaxing and being pampered sounding like hard work, rather than a deeply insulting remark about Tricia's looks.

I noticed a definite uncertainty in her voice as she bravely struggled on.

"Thursday would be better. Would you be able to phone on Thursday morning to let me know a time?"

"No problem at all. You mentioned the weekend's a birthday treat for your husband? Just in case he answers the phone,

it's not a surprise is it? I don't want to be the one to break it to him."

With hindsight, "break it to him" may not have been the best way to describe mentioning a weekend away with Tricia, especially as a follow-on to my questioning her ability to look good for it.

Her voice was definitely beginning to waver; I had to explain quickly before she called the cattery in town.

"I'm not doing very well here, am I? I'm not saying a weekend away with you would be terrible or anything, ha ha… I just mean… um…"

Somehow, Tricia forced herself to finalise the booking. However, I'm fairly sure she told her cat Bertha all about my impudent remarks, because over the course of the weekend, Bertha tore me to pieces.

Bertha was an "insecure sort of cat" who could be a bit feisty

I arrived at Tricia's home on Friday evening, immediately spotting a picture of Tricia on the wall. I was relieved to see that she was an extremely nice-looking woman. My comments probably went straight over her head.

At that moment, Bertha went straight over my head. I'd been warned that Bertha was an "insecure sort of cat" and never to corner her as she could be "a bit feisty".

Obviously the first thing I did was corner her, but I had absolutely no idea she was sitting on a chair below Tricia's picture.

Bertha's first leap for freedom took her straight up my right arm, clawing her way to my shoulder, which she used as a launch-pad to the open space behind me, virtually scalping me in the process.

As I tended to my wounds I realised there was an important lesson to be learned… I should never, ever, be allowed to speak to normal people. Especially not ones with violent cats.

MARCHING ORDERS!

Who'd have thought the pet of sports stars would be such a vocal disciplinarian?

I 've been looking after a celebrity kitten this week. To look at her, you don't instantly notice any particular star quality but she is actually quite an important feline, belonging as she does to a pair of international sports stars.

When I took on Poppy's care, I only knew that her owners play hockey and this takes them away on trips quite regularly. I knew this because their opening email was entitled "Kitten-Hockey."

This sounded like a pretty cruel sport to me, but I soon got the gist of what was required and two weeks later I was visiting Poppy at home while her owners were away.

The first thing I noticed about Poppy was that she didn't look much like a kitten, though I think she'd have every right to claim kittenhood under the "less than a year old" rule. The second thing I noticed was that, although coming from a sporting family, she's not that sporty. In fact, she doesn't really move that much.

Poppy directs everything I do by bellowing instructions

Poppy prefers to stand on kitchen work surfaces, shouting. She does this from the moment I walk into the house. Poppy directs every single thing I do by simply standing bolt upright

57

and bellowing instructions at me.

Each meow has a specific meaning and it's all a bit intimidating. "FEED ME!", "STROKE ME!", "GET YOUR HANDS OUT OF MY LITTER TRAY, YOU FILTHY PIG!"

I just admitted to being intimidated by a kitten – now there's another string to my macho bow.

After one of these exercise yard drills, I was driving away from Poppy's house, still a bit shaken, when I switched on the radio only to hear one of her owners talking. I learned in the next few moments that I'd misunderstood his hockey habits to be a hobby. He's actually captain of the Great Britain Hockey Team.

Captain… hmm, that must involve a bit of shouting – maybe Poppy had picked up some of her owner's sporting attributes after all.

I then discovered that her "mum" is in the GB women's team. Wow! No other kitten in the country can have the same claim to fame as Poppy – she is indeed Kitten Hockey.

My next stop was at a local vets, where I had to collect a bag of prescription cat food for my next client, also a kitten, but a proper one – a small one. I definitely think the bag could have been labelled a little more carefully. Speciality Diet Dry Cat Food – with Chicken, Kitten. Surely the word "kitten" was in completely the wrong place there. I certainly hope so. Unless, I thought, this is the sort of thing that happens after a particularly vigorous game of kitten hockey?

On the subject of sporting stars, I also occasionally look after a cat for Louise Sugden, a member of the Great Britain Paralympic Basketball team. When Louise acquired her cat from a pet rescue charity she already had a name, and Louise didn't think it would be right to change it. That name is Molly.

So there you have it – catsitter to the stars! Not only do I work for sporting heroes, I also feed Molly Sugden.

A STICKY SITUATION

It seems cats just can't resist turning Chris into something resembling Quasimodo

My wife Lorraine is forever forcing me to "look after myself." Probably noting my failure to look after rabbits particularly effectively, she must feel the need to keep an eye on the situation. This enforced self-mindfulness can involve anything from putting a coat on in -10 degrees (she puts my reluctance to do so down to a Geordie gene in my heritage) to occasionally eating vegetables (really, I much prefer eating things that eat vegetables) and applying various creams and moisturisers before "it's too late". I'm concerned about what exactly happens when it's too late, but I resist the horrible oily stuff at all costs.

Every now and then though, Lorraine catches me totally unaware and slaps huge blobs of some cream or other onto my cheeks or hands. It was my hands she collared the other day, with the strict order "just rub it in and stop complaining".

Well, that was easier said than done. No amount of hand rubbing would make it disappear. As I continued with my laborious task, my tortoiseshell Cat Jojo jumped onto my lap and demanded to be stroked. Obviously, this was something I couldn't do while covered

Stroking Jojo with **hand cream** on, I found, was not a **good idea**

in sticky cream, but as her meows grew angry, I did so anyway, instantly regretting it.

One stroke and I looked like I was wearing a pair of wolf-man gloves, but one stroke was never going to be enough for Jojo, and realising she'd be getting no more, she turned haughtily on her heels and tail-flicked me in the eye. It was a spot-on strike. I grabbed at my running eye and was immediately stunned by the sting of two tons of hand cream plus fur.

Jojo, initially delighted to have caught me with a crafty hit, now jumped 3 feet in the air as l howled in pain, claw swiping me across the nose on the way down like a Kung Fu Panda ninja.

Now I was in a real mess, hunched over, bleeding from a gash across my nose, one eye wide open, the other half closed and streaming, like Quasimodo from the Hunchback of Notre Dame. Lorraine walked back into the room at that very moment and stopped in her tracks.

"The hand-cream," I rasped, holding my outstretched hairy hands towards Esmeralda – em, Lorraine – who recoiled in revulsion. She'd only left me two minutes ago, and all I had to do was rub in some moisturiser.

Believe it or not, this type of horrific transformation has happened to me before. On a catsitting pre-visit to meet a cat named Henry, the owner left the room to make a coffee while Henry and I got acquainted. Within seconds my ridiculously excitable new feline friend thrust his head into my face so hard I saw swirling stars. Moments later, he claw-kneaded my neck with joyous ferocity.

The stunned owner returned to find an unrecognisable man with scratches around his neck and a rapidly blacking eye…

DESPERATE MEASURES

Chris's temporary deafness has some far-reaching effects...

After a recent ear infection, which I though had cleared up, I was struck down with another one. It was a short-lived virus, but left me temporarily partially deaf in both ears. My doctor's response was to render me totally deaf by ordering me to continually pour warm olive oil into my ears ahead of a syringing. So it was that I was consigned to a strange world where the only sound was the gentle lapping of olive oil waves, and the only sights an assortment of shouting faces.

I was unaware of an ambulance, sirens blaring, right behind me

The effects on the household of my sudden loss of hearing were dramatic. My wife Lorraine was the first to suffer because, as everybody knows, 90 percent of married life involves shouting "what?" at each other from other rooms. This marital tradition suddenly became impossible for Lorraine. She'd start a conversation from a distant room and receive only an eerie silence in response. Our marriage was suddenly a sham.

My daughter, being a teenager, was simply angered at my inability to hear anything at all.

"Would you get angry at a disabled person for not being able to

ZZZZZZZZZ

63

walk?" I said, attempting to point out the unfairness of her attitude. It is of course impossible to reach the moral high ground with a teenager and I ended up hanging my head as I lip-read the words "How dare you compare needing your ears syringed to somebody suffering a lifelong disability!"

Even the pets noticed the difference. Bodmin the cat found that shouting at the fridge no longer resulted in my appearing from nowhere to feed him chicken, and began to worry that his caterwaul had become obsolete. Jojo, perplexed that meowing full blast in my face now failed to wake me during the night, resorted to dive bombing me from the top of the wardrobe. Billie the rabbit discovered that slamming her Thumper-like back foot down hard on the hutch floor no longer stalled my approach and found the only way to stop me removing old hay was by biting me. My lack of hearing was becoming painful on all fronts, though Billie's partner Ted noticed no difference – but then he doesn't notice anything at all.

Out of all the people annoyed by my deafness though, nobody could have been more so than a couple of members of our local hospital staff.

While leaving the ear-clinic after being told I'd need another week of warm olive oil before they'd be prepared to squirt water into my ears, I walked glumly down the hospital drive, lost in a sea of self-pity and totally unaware that there was an ambulance with a blaring siren right behind me. I led the ambulance all the way down that drive like a solemn undertaker leading a hearse.

I may not have heard the siren, but I certainly read the lips of the driver as he mounted a kerb to go round me. I could say I've been called worse things, but I really don't think I have… 🐾

HARD OF HEARING

Chris's additional communication difficulties continue… but relief is at hand

Carrying on from my last story, after failing to convince my local hospital to syringe my ears before they were ready to be syringed, I found myself facing another week of almost total deafness. After initial household anger at my lack of hearing – and I quote my teenage daughter Maya here, "IF YOU CAN'T

Jojo began jumping at me in the way Cato attacked Clouseau

HEAR, THEN DON'T SPEAK!" – both humans and pets became used to my situation and began taking advantage of it.

Maya would claim to have definitely received a "yes" to her chocolate bar request when I could have sworn she'd asked if I'd like a coffee.

My wife Lorraine could chat on the phone about my shortcomings while I sat smiling benignly, wondering why Maya was taking so long with the coffee. Jojo the cat suddenly started jumping at me from all angles, in much the way Cato attacked Clouseau in the Pink Panther movies, delighted by my inability to hear her un-ninja-like approaches.

Meanwhile, Barry from a few doors down discovered my condition in the most ridiculous of circumstances. Emerging from

our cars at the same moment, we shouted our hellos. Then Barry shouted again.

"I can't hear you, I've gone deaf!" I bellowed, pointing at my ears. Barry seemed to understand as he responded by pointing at his own ears… but then he yelled again.

"No," I shouted, "I'm deaf!"

With that Barry shouted something else and began walking towards me. I walked towards him. As we reached one another, both still shouting, I realised Barry was trying to tell me that he'd gone deaf. It turned out he'd had the same ear infection, and was also smuggling olive oil within his auditory canal. We laughed in mutual understanding, each said something the other didn't hear, and went on our way.

Then, on Tuesday, the most wonderful thing happened. I went to the ear clinic, carefully on the lookout for enraged ambulance drivers and, after a brief inspection, was deemed all clear to have pints of water shot into both ears. As the water seeped away, I sat up unsteadily, and suddenly became aware of all sorts of weird sounds – the sounds of everyday life. I could hear!

"IS THAT OK?" said the nurse, her voice sounding like a cannon going off two feet from my right ear.

"Yes," I whispered, wondering how I'd never realised the world was such a loud place. I could even hear a clock ticking. It was fantastic!

Off I went on my cat-sitting rounds, in a state of near ecstasy. It proved a strange, very loud day. One cat mewed behind me and I almost jumped six feet over the sofa. Another hissed and I went looking for a gas leak.

Maybe the best part, though, was arriving home and hearing my daughter tell her friend that I'm a "good dad". She wouldn't have said that in a million years if she'd known I could hear her… 🐾

PITCH IMPERFECT

Chris recalls his past experience of trying to erect a gazebo with the unwanted help of one of his furry friends...

I received orders from Lorraine to erect a gazebo the other day. Amazingly, I managed to do so without incidents or mishaps whatsoever. So that's the end of this week's column. Hope you enjoyed it.

However, it reminded of an earlier gazebo assembly, and a certain cat's "help". You guessed it – Brum. The earlier gazebo was of a much more complicated design than the pop-up affair I've just completed. It came in a flat pack, and as with most flat-pack items, the assembly instructions were an exercise in disinformation. Having decoded the first section, a huge skeletal framework of interconnecting poles gradually formed around me. Or fell around me mainly.

The poles were all slightly too short. Every time I connected one, another fell out three metres behind me. My constant companion Brum sat on our garden wall, gazing down at me, ears pinned back in annoyance at all the metallic clangs as each pole hit the ground.

Finally, even though the connected poles were pretty precarious, I hauled a large fitted cover over the bars. Having shrouded myself three times, it eventually slipped into place. At last, I stood proudly inspecting the new white roof above my head. I stopped for a moment and smiled at the twitchy eared silhouette of my tabby

Read Chris Pascoe's column every week!

Short stories, health experts, interviews, great recipes, fashion and beauty buys

On Sale Every Tuesday

A FEAST OF DELIGHTFUL READING!

friend as he washed atop the wall, clearly visible through the thin fabric covering. All that remained was to secure the covering to the poles.

My smile faded as the silhouette started doing something it really shouldn't. Its backside raised and wiggled, its nose pointed towards me. The stupid cat was about to leap down onto the new white rooftop that had suddenly appeared before him. Brum's jump preparation routine gave me a little time, but not enough.

As I lurched towards him everything seemed to go into slow-motion. I raised a helpless hand to the sky as the shadow of an airborne cat loomed across the white canvas above me.

Then there was mayhem. The unsecured roof caved in about my ears, metal clattered around my feet and a gazebo-cloaked loony-cat smacked into my face.

The shadow of an airborne cat loomed across the gazebo

All this seemed to annoy Brum. I found myself embroiled in a fist fight with a 3-by-4 white sheet as Brum fought to free himself. As ripping sounds joined the general cacophony of clanging poles, I realised he'd broken through.

As suddenly as it began, everything was still. I sat in absolute dejection, wearing my gazebo palace. There was a scratching noise and a corner lifted. A scruffy tabby face appeared and looked at me. I stared back for a few moments and laughed, despite myself. With a bit of determined squirming, Brum forced his way fully inside our makeshift tent, sat on my lap and began purring.

And that was that. A man and a cat at peace with one another again, beneath a 3-by-4 white sheet, amid the ruins of an almost-gazebo.

A Day In The Life
of a CATSITTER!

Twenty-four hours of moggies and mishaps

When My Weekly asked me to write a 'day in the life' diary piece for the centre pages of this book, I have to admit I first thought I could get away with summarising my usual day in five lines:

7.30am: Get up

7.30am – 1pm: Do something very stupid

1 – 2pm: Lunch

2 – 11pm: Humiliate myself

11pm: Go to bed

But, apparently I need to go a little more in depth than that, so to give a good example of my typical day, I decided to make some notes over the last week. Wednesday proved to be more 'typical' than the rest, so it's Wednesday that we have here:

7.15am Virtually fell out of bed to the sound of our Alexa device inexplicably talking loudly to herself in the kitchen. She does that from time to time. I'm just glad they managed to fix her middle-of-the-night-manic-laughing-glitch… that was disturbing.

7.35am Onto the computer, armed with a cup of tea and a piece of toast, to befuddle some customers with a few predictive-text email replies. This time round, I don't think I managed to answer any 'have a nice day' wishes with 'thanks, you tool' rather than 'you too' but you never know.

8am Gave the rabbits their breakfast

8.20am Ted noticed his breakfast

Chris's life revolves round all things cat!

Billie and Ted

8.30am Ted seemed to remember he'd noticed his breakfast a while back

8.35am Took Maya to school. I've learnt never to speak to Maya en-route - she doesn't like it.

9am – Drove to my first catsitting visit of the day. More cups of tea with three happy kittens bouncing all over me, attempting to spill my tea

Cats always pay attention to Chris. Not!

9.45 – 10am Washed the kittens' food bowls, emptied their litter tray, swept the floor. Ready to leave.

10.01am Snagged the bin bag on the way out, sending a thousand tiny grains of cat litter in all directions, much to the delight of the kittens who gleefully set about chasing every grain up and down the hall's wooden floor.

10.02 -10.15am Swept the floor... again

10.30am Arrived at my next catsitting, and spent quite some time watching Donald the soundly sleeping elderly tabby snoring at me.

11am Donald vanished into thin air before my very eyes. Well, it seemed that way anyway. I finally realised I'd nodded off to sleep too, and Donald had long since departed through his catflap. I don't think he likes me as much as I like him.

11.30am My next catsitting visit. Nothing happened at all, so this in itself is noteworthy

12.30pm Arrived at the home of a very good customer who hasn't been in the UK long, and whilst her language learning skills have been truly impressive, her written English can sometimes be a bit confusing. Nevertheless, I was surprised to find a post-it in the kitchen saying:

'Hi Chris. Charlie not been out all day, so when you get here, give him a kicking please.' Bearing in mind this was the same customer who once texted me saying that her son had 'done a massive sick so please send some cat pictures' (she was actually referring to her son being homesick and missing his cat) this sort of message wasn't really a surprise, but it did present a problem. Should I check the notes meaning...or just kick him? I decided that, given that I'd never before been asked to assault a customer's cat on arrival, and not really liking the idea, I'd give the owner a ring.

I'm glad I checked. It didn't, as I suspected might be the case in a round about sort of way, mean 'kick him out', but instead referred to setting up (or booting up?) his microchip catflap to allow him controlled outdoor access. Of course it did - anyone should've known kick the cat means reset the catflap.

1.30pm Home for lunch. Lorraine was out, the cats and rabbits were asleep, so I sat eating a sandwich and staring at the goldfish. This is an indicator of my high-octane existence.

2 – 3pm Decided to write my My Weekly Column

3.30pm Stopped staring at the fish, and started writing, but not about fish.

Do they inspire Chris to write?

5.30pm Collected Maya from school, later than usual because she'd been playing volleyball. Readers of my column may remember that while Maya's volleyball position is Setter, and her friend's have glamorously named positions such as Spiker and Libero, my volleyball position is...Tosser.

And that last line, I feel, closes my day's diary entries in about the most typical way possible.

Every Day's A Disaster

The hapless Chris seems to court trouble.
Whether it's animals or humans, he seems
to have the unhappy knack of getting into
hot water at every possibility. But it does
give him the chance to tell hilarious stories
in his weekly column in My Weekly.
Join him as he relates some of his more
memorable catastrophes.

Every Day's A Disaster

HIT AND WALK!

The impact was far from the most worrying element of this encounter…

I recently wrote a book involving a slightly chaotic pub crawl around the major battlefields of the English Civil War. I won't cheapen and belittle myself by naming the book in an attempt to sell more copies (Death, Destruction and a Packet of Peanuts, available now in all good bookshops) but I thought I'd tell you about my brush with death while researching the book.

I was run over in possibly the lowest-speed road accident of all time.

On that particular day I was very excited to be visiting Newbury, Berkshire (and it'll be a long time before you hear somebody say that again), scene of some historically momentous Cavalier v Roundhead events back in the 1600s. Upon parking at the side of a busy road, I let Peter Ilic and his dog Dave (my sidekicks throughout my Civil War travels) out of the car and watched them run, panting and happy, into the nearest pub.

I surveyed my surroundings. This busy, built-up, traffic choked area looked very little like a bloody battlefield now, but I was delighted to spot a huge Civil War monument on the opposite side of the road. So delighted in fact, that I stepped straight out in front of oncoming traffic without a useful thought in my head. The car that hit me didn't stand a chance. Fortunately for me it was being driven by a lady of advanced years at a speed approaching three miles per hour.

79

I waved an apology, and heartfelt thanks to her for having the foresight to drive so slowly on a major highway. By the beeps emanating from behind her, I guessed this appreciation was shared.

I carried on across the road, aware the beeps were getting louder. The elderly lady had abandoned her vehicle in the middle of the road and was walking towards me at an alarmingly slow pace.

"I'm OK," I called. "No damage done! Sorry."

She kept on coming.

"Shouldn't you go back to your car?" I shouted over the cacophony of car horns.

She kept on coming.

"You're blocking the road, you know?"

Finally she reached me and looked me square in the face.

"Oooh, sorry love, I thought you were Jean Muckridge's boy! You're not a Muckridge, are you?"

"Eh – no," I replied, aware that car doors were now opening and that a great many angry people were heading my way. Suddenly and unexpectedly, I'd made the area look much more like the battlefield I'd originally been hoping for. "I'm really sorry for stepping out like that. You really should go back to your car you know?"

She had abandoned her car right in the middle of the road

She waved my suggestion aside. "Well," she said, "I'd have put my life on you being a Muckridge."

I reassured her I wasn't and she finally turned back towards her car. Then, just when I thought my ordeal was over, she called over her shoulder, "All you Muckridges are bloody idiots. Stepping out like that! Pah."

LAID BACK

When it comes to aeroplane seating, the decline of the recliner is to be celebrated

When it comes to aeroplane seating, the decline of the recliner is to be celebrated.

I read recently that many airlines are thinking of doing away with reclining seats. While most people would have glanced over this tiny news snippet without raising so much as an eyebrow, I actually clenched my fist in a victory salute and gave a loud cheer, so startling the extremely edgy cat that I'd forgotten was sitting on my lap, resulting in minor leg wounds and multiple slashes to my trouser pocket.

Although the phasing out of reclining seats seems an extremely unlikely thing to cheer about, I have a certain amount of justification. I have a deep-seated fear (excuse the pun) of aeroplane reclining seats, as a result of two unfortunate incidents…

My first recliner-altercation came when my daughter Maya was just a tiny baby on her first ever flight, a trip to the island of Menorca. We approached the flight with some trepidation, being first time parents and still slightly terrified of our brand new daughter (actually, she's still slightly terrifying).

I was Maya's chief nappy changer at the time, due to Lorraine having conveniently discovered she had an allergy to baby-wipes (she claims to suffer the very same extreme allergic reaction to washing- up liquid, furniture polish and kitchen cleaner). So when that dreaded moment came, 35,000 feet above France, Maya was thrust into my arms and Lorraine began rummaging through the hand-luggage for all the necessary equipment.

The queue for the toilet stretched halfway up the aisle

and it was at this moment that I made a wonderful discovery… the seat's flip-down tray made a perfect nappy changing unit once a changing mat was laid on it.

All was going well until, suddenly, the seat in front reclined at a sharp angle. Both baby and partly removed nappy rolled straight onto my lap, with a very light thud in the baby's case, and with a gut-wrenching splat in the other.

Both baby and nappy rolled into my lap with a squelching sound

I was suddenly in about the worst possible mess any man could be in on a crowded aeroplane and wearing a pair of light coloured trousers. My subsequent interminable wait in the toilet queue will stay with me forever.

Recliner incident two came around five years later and, while much more fragrant, was no less embarrassing. I'd just reached the last question on my crossword puzzle when I dropped both my pen and puzzle book on the floor. I ducked down beneath my seat-tray and had to stretch quite a way under the seat in front of me to reach my runaway pen. The occupant of this seat chose that very moment to go into full reclining mode. The bulk of the seat sailed back over my head and I found myself completely trapped beneath my own tray.

My desperate attempts to alert the woman in the seat beside me to my predicament were futile. She glanced down at my face peering up at her from close to my own feet, seemed to decide I was a bit odd, turned her iPod volume up, and closed her eyes. I was only released after she reported me for tugging on her ankles.

So now you understand. Goodbye reclining airline seats – and good riddance! 🐾

RADIO GAGA!

The sight of the on-air light sends a nervous Chris into interview orbit...

One of the biggest problems of having a book released is that your publisher then expects you to talk to people. Apparently, somewhat bewilderingly, the publishing powers-that-be seemed to think that a man who'd happily sit in a small room and write 250 pages about his own cat would be someone people would like to hear speak.

Thus it was that Hodder & Stoughton arranged, to my horror, a schedule of radio and press interviews for me. From stroking cats and cleaning out litter trays all day, I was suddenly whisked around London in a black cab, with my own publicist at my side. I was totally out of my depth.

My first appointment was with Smooth Radio, then called Saga, in a small first floor studio. The resident DJ took the time to run through the sort of questions he'd be asking. He also advised that I keep my answers fairly short, but light and informative, and leave it to him to keep the conversation running smoothly.

I apologised and assured the DJ that I was back in control now

I'm not quite sure what happened next. All I remember is the DJ asking the first question, glancing at the red ON AIR sign and going into some kind of blind panic.

I went off on a babbling five-minute tirade at breakneck speed, laughing at the end of every single sentence and totally unable

85

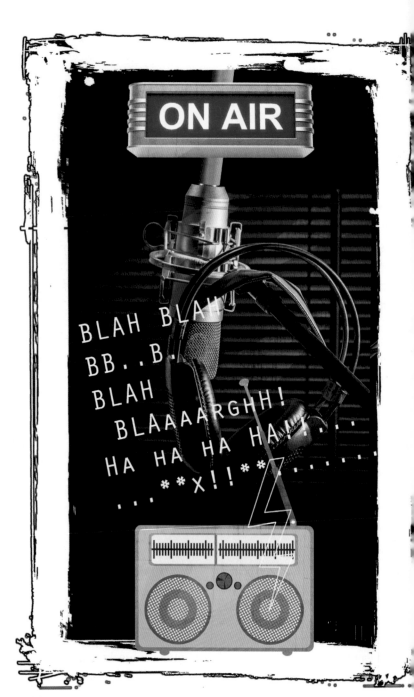

to stop. The publicist holding her head in her hands and the DJ's finger-across-throat gestures should have suggested things weren't going well.

Finally, I realised my microphone was off and Cool for Cats had replaced my crazed voice on London's airwaves. The DJ stared at me in astonishment.

"OK," he announced. "We're going to need to change things radically here. Remember, keep those answers much shorter, none of that loud shouting and chuckling."

I apologised and assured him I was back in control now. He slapped me on the back, returned to his chair and on popped that dreaded ON AIR sign again.

"So Chris, these are exciting times for you. What's it like to be published for the first time? I always think it must be the most incredible experience to walk into a book shop and see your own book, the book you spent all that time planning and writing, up there on the shelves, with your name staring back at you. Were you totally on cloud nine when you first saw it?"

"Yes."

Silence. After a couple of hand-waves, the despairing presenter quickly recovered.

"OK, fantastic stuff. We'll chat some more with Chris after this next song." The DJ stared at me and shook his head. "Right, Chris, we're going to have to go back to your first approach. Say whatever you like, but try to speak a lot slower, don't ramble and just… tone it all down, OK? You OK with that? Chris?"

I smiled and nodded. I felt I was getting to grips with this radio stuff now. And it all went very well. I became one of the few people ever to swear on Saga Radio.

SPARKS FLY

Chris's good deed at a fireworks display is taken completely the wrong way

Fireworks displays are traditionally happy and joyous events, and so aren't the sort of place you'd expect some moron to start a fight. So I'd just like to explain how I once started a fight at a fireworks display…

It all began because it was the wrong kind of wind that night. It was blowing directly over the crowd and, instead of tiny embers drifting harmlessly away, they mainly landed on us.

I first became aware of the problem when my friend suddenly clapped a hand over his eye, mumbled something and rushed towards the exit. A few moments later a glowing orange ball gently alighted upon a raincoat directly in front of me and immediately started melting it.

My reaction was impulsive – I began slapping the raincoat as hard as I could without considering for a moment that there was someone inside it.

The raincoat's occupant stiffened, slowly turned and then without a word, attempted to punch me in the face. His first punch was a wild in-swinger, just missing my left ear…but to the wrong side, smacking me straight in the left eye. His second punch became entangled in my hood.

As I tried to pull away, my hood now over my face, people all around began trying to separate us. They didn't need to do this, as I was actually trying to run off, but they were in my way.

I repeatedly tried to shout what had happened, but nobody could hear a word, mainly because Airbomb Repeaters are much noisier than me, and also because everybody was shouting "Break it up,

lads!"

My unexpected opponent had no intention of backing down, his confidence in victory no doubt bolstered by his assailant's frenzied attack being so thoroughly useless. If somebody came up and began jumping up and down girly-slapping your shoulders, you'd be confident too.

By now the tannoy announcer had spotted the melée and was also getting involved. "Security! Crowd disturbance near Binky's

"Security! Crowd disturbance near Binky's burger van..."

burger van. Please attend."

It all fizzled out before security arrived, with my sparring partner and I ushered in opposite directions in a sea of bodies.

I met my friend an hour later in the pub. Neither of us could open our left eye.

I recently told my daughter Maya and her school friend Jess about this long-ago incident, and while receiving the traditional teenage grunt from Maya, I was surprised to see Jess light up in sudden excited animation – she'd recently been told a similar type of story, in which the individual concerned caused shock to all around him by seemingly engaging in an act of senseless aggression.

The teller had been the girls' mutual school friend Megan, and it all happened at a local petting zoo named The Goat Centre. Due to a misunderstanding, a group of stunned children, including Megan herself, watched a man suddenly and for no apparent reason throw a full bag of goat food straight into a donkey's face.

Maya and I laughed politely, and said nothing… 🐾

THE DEAD ZONE

Chris has a spooky experience in a wooded copse in Chalgrove...

Researching a book I wrote about a pub crawl through the English Civil War Battlefields, not only did I haunt an awful lot of pubs, I was also left haunted on a number of occasions – not least by an eerie clump of trees in a the middle of a deserted field.

I first heard about the Dead Zone in a pub close to the 1643 battlefield of Chalgrove. My constant companion on research trips, Pete, was adhering to his research procedure of getting drunk and pumping locals for helpful information, while I followed my own procedure – sitting at a nearby table feeling conspicuous.

It was at the very moment an elderly man started telling Pete about a spooky area of Chalgrove where no animals will ever go, that I realised there was a man under my table. I just looked down, and saw a face looking up at me.

The closer I got, the more I felt the urge to turn and run

"Aargghh!" I yelled. The bar conversation stopped. I looked down in horror, the man looked up in horror. Then he crawled backwards and ran from the pub.

Pete and his acquaintance shrugged and resumed their

conversation. As I sat in shock, I just about heard the name and whereabouts of the Dead Zone over the thumping of my own heart.

"Eh, excuse me," I finally interrupted, "What just happened? The man under the table?"

"He likes legs," answered the elderly man, and with that the matter was closed. Pete chuckled and war-talk resumed. Chalgrove was becoming a stranger place by the second.

Two weeks later, I stood in a damp field and stared at a copse of trees. Obviously I did – I believe everything semi-drunk people in pubs tell me. I sat on my coat and stared for ages, scanning the woodland with binoculars. At one point a squirrel came and sat beside me.

Thus far I'd treated the whole thing as an exercise to disprove a silly story but, surprisingly, I could see no movement in the copse at all. I was also taken aback to see a bird change direction mid-flight, seemingly to avoid it. After a while, I became satisfied that the area was indeed devoid of life. It was time to experiment by placing a mammal in there. Being a mammal, I nominated myself and began walking towards the trees.

I'm sure it was all in my head but the closer I got, the more I felt an urge to turn and run. Then, as I reached the edge of the copse, I jumped in shock – the eerie silence had been broken by the loud honk of my car horn, obviously beeped by the ever impatient Pete. I stepped forward and the horn began beeping repeatedly. I suddenly wondered if Pete was in need of help. I began running back to the car but as I reached it the beeps stopped and I remembered something quite significant. Pete wasn't with me that day.

I glanced back at the copse, shivered, and decided some unknowns will just have to stay unknown. 🐾

WILD FRONTIER

Theme parks, safari parks – a safe, enjoyable family day out… for some

Although bitter experience over the years should have taught me otherwise I finally braved a return visit to a well known theme park recently.

The last time I'd been to this park, an attraction broke down and we found ourselves in a long line of people walking out through a dark tunnel behind animatronic dragons, looking at their backsides full of wires and levers. It kind of spoiled the magic.

Yet here I was again, ready to face all the park could throw at me. We started with a nice gentle safari truck ride. This wasn't a "ride" in the true sense. It really was just a truck, driving through enclosures of real animals – none likely to have exposed mechanical levers hanging out of their rear ends.

However, I had concerns. I'd recently watched the movie Jurassic World so my overall opinion of the safety of safari attractions was at an all-time low – and with my track record with the tiniest and tamest of animals…

As we trundled along in the open truck, to the sounds of a recorded commentary telling us, for the purposes of entertainment, that we were in mortal danger, I relaxed slightly as I watched giraffes milling around without an ounce of interest in us.

I was actually enjoying myself! I even spotted a herd of rhinoceros, thankfully safely on the other side of a robust fence. Wouldn't want to be in with that bunch!

94

The truck driver took a left and headed straight for the rhinos. A gate with warning lights suddenly lifted and in we drove, into the herd. The biggest rhino looked up and immediately singled me out.

I smiled nervously. He glared malevolently back.

I raised a hand. His eyes visibly narrowed.

Suddenly another rhino nuzzled his face and, after one last glare, he turned away. I'm convinced the second rhino whispered something in his ear – along the lines of "Leave it, Dave, he's not worth it".

The truck trundled on through a waterfall, the frantic commentator now sure we were goners, and back to base, home and dry.

The biggest rhino looked up and immediately singled me out

If you ever happen to go on this safari ride, the worst seat is front-left just behind the driver. While everyone else stays dry, freezing waterfall water pours from a puddle in the overhead canopy and straight down the neck of whoever's in that seat. I was in that seat. Unable to move under my safety-bar, I spent the next five minutes as a human water-feature – water streaming into my collar and down over my lap.

As I eventually climbed from the truck, the next group stared at my trousers in surprise. It seemed the ride was more nerve-wracking than they'd expected…

THINGS THAT GO BUMP...

Three strikes, and hapless Chris finds himself… well, not out, but certainly in a tight corner with an apparently stroppy builder.

People keep driving cars at me lately. While this might not surprise some readers of my column, it's becoming a bit of a problem.

I've been involved in three car crashes in three months. Amazingly, on every occasion I was stationary at the time. If this had been on the fast lane of the M6, I could understand it, but no. I was hit twice while waiting to turn right, and on the third occasion I'd just parked my car when an elderly chap reversed into me at high speed. This was a rear-end-shunt with a difference. It was the rear end doing the shunting.

As a result, I've spent most of the last three months in body-shop courtesy cars. It was while in one of these courtesy cars that I became involved in a bit of an incident.

Spotting me, he clambered down his ladder and began running

I was pulling out of a customer's gate when a huge burly builder, halfway up a ladder three doors down, spotted me, clambered down his ladder and began running full pelt at me. This had the makings of yet another road-traffic accident – it was just lucky for

me he didn't have a car on him at the time.

Stopping at my window he stared in, panting, so close that my window steamed up. I slowly wound it down and politely asked if I could help?

"You too dense!" he shouted in response.

That was a bit unfair, I thought. He didn't even know me. If he did, fair enough.

"Um, pardon?" I asked

"You too dense?" he repeated, this time looking me up and down and then staring at my empty passenger seat. Was he overestimating the number of people in my car by 100%?

Just when I thought his next line would be "C'mon, I'll take you both on, the pair of yous, you and your fancy passenger seat!" he tapped my door and said patiently, "Dense, mate, you, do you do dense? I need some dense doing."

Then it hit me. My courtesy car was emblazoned with the name Panelcraft Car Body Repairs. He thought I was a panel-beater, and that I "did dents".

Noticing his van parked down the road, I could see exactly why he was asking.

"Ah, no, sorry." I laughed. "It's not my car, it's a courtesy car. I never know what car I'm in to be honest, I've had three accidents in three months and…"

"Ha!" he suddenly shouted, grinning. "My mistake, mate!"

With that, he turned heel and began pacing away. Halfway back to his ladder he stopped and looked back over his shoulder.

"Three accidents in three months, mate?"

"Yeah, I don't know why but…" I shrugged.

"Clumsy sod!" he guffawed, and with that he was gone.

MONKEY BUSINESS!

As a test of intellect, the quiz was never going to be a roaring success...

I was watching a rerun of a popular quiz show the other day. While this type of afternoon behaviour goes a long way to explaining why my new book is two years past its deadline, it did enable me to witness what was surely one of the most stunning quiz answers in history.

Quiz Master: What ancient civilisation built the British road known as Watling Street?

Contestant: Apes.

What!? Apes?? Now, whichever way you look at it, this answer goes way beyond what could be taken as a very bad guess. There's so much to take from it that it's difficult to know where to start, but the main thing has to be that this contestant clearly believed there to have been, at some time in the distant past, an ancient civilisation of apes who ruled Britain and built good roads.

You learn something new every day

How did she ever manage to form an opinion like that? I sat and pondered this question for quite some time and the only conclusion I could reach was that at some point in her childhood she watched the original Planet of the Apes movies and believed them to be documentaries.

Having said all that, my own record in quizzes has never been

great. Totally panicked and temporarily befuddled during a team quiz competition a while back, despite knowing the correct answer (Ronald Reagan) I managed to achieve the following:

Quiz Master: Who was the President of America from 1981 to 1989?

Pascoe, Muppet University: Ronald MacDonald.

The quiz master's mouth actually dropped open, as my teammates shook their heads incredulously. Mind you, I had absolutely no complaints about the Happy Meal I was ceremoniously presented with at our next match.

Neither was I the only one in that particular team of "winners" to come up with the occasional ill thought-out answer...

Quiz Master: Where is the quietest place on Earth?

Teammate 1: The Moon.

Great answer. Wrong planet. OK, that also made me sound a bit thick... wrong celestial body then.

Quiz Master: At what battle did Admiral Horatio Nelson die?

Teammate 2: The Battle of Britain.

Yes, because as everybody knows, Horatio Nelson was a World War 2 Spitfire pilot.

I'm sure this will come as a bit of a shock to many readers out there, but we haven't won that many trophies.

Right, all this quiz-talk's got me in the mood for more – let's see what's on TV today. Or maybe I should get back to writing the book?

Hmm, probably the latter – the publisher suddenly stopped chasing me a while back so they may well have given me up for dead.

Incidentally, checking back, the quietest place on Earth is actually the Anechoic Chamber at Orfield Laboratories, Minneapolis. And all this time I'd believed it to be the Sea of Tranquillity. You learn something new every day. 🐾

TROUBLE IN STORE

Chris gets more than he bargained for at his local supermarket

One of my local supermarkets is a lot more confrontational than most in our area. The trouble starts the moment you walk into the foyer. From nowhere you're greeted by a recorded child-like voice shouting, "Hello. Do you want to have a go?"

That's not a good start is it? One foot inside the door and a disembodied voice challenges you to a fight. You realise after a few seconds that the voice actually emanates from a kiddies ride with a chirpy face painted onto a mini aeroplane named Jim. Surely there must be better ways of asking for 50p.

So now he's suggesting that I look homeless! Keep calm...

The real problems start when you reach the till. On this particular occasion I admit I chanced the "five items or fewer" till with six items, but they were all tiny bags of Dreamies Cat Treats and I was holding them in one hand.

"Did you read the sign? You've too many items."

"But they're all the same item and they're on a BOGOF. You only need to scan one of them. I can hold the others."

"That's not my fault."

103

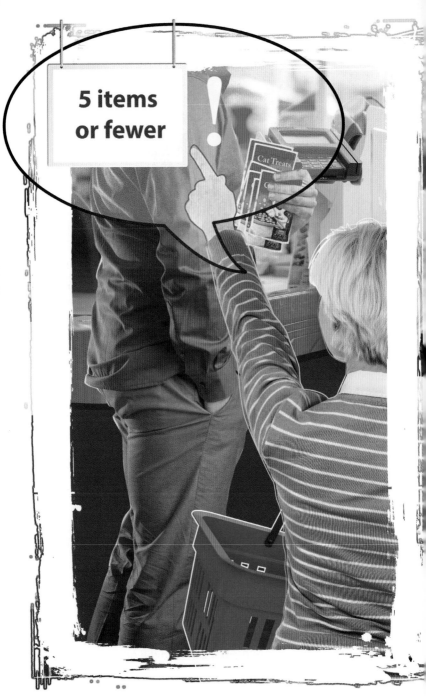

Not her fault? I wasn't trying to apportion blame. I just wanted the Dreamies.

"But…"

"I don't make the rules."

So after a 10 minute queue at the trolley till without a trolley, I finally managed to pay and found the BOGOF actually worked out as "buy one, get one". A BOGO – not nearly as good.

This supermarket is also the only one in town that consistently gets all its prices completely wrong. I feel sure they do this to make sure you don't leave without first being able to have an argument at the customer service desk. Do you remember the Monty Python sketch where people paid to go into a room to have an argument? That pretty much sums up this supermarket's customer service desk.

"Hi, I just bought these Dreamies but the BOGOF didn't work."

"You don't have a receipt. How do I know you haven't just picked those up and brought them straight here."

"What? I wouldn't do that," I said, pulling out my receipt, actually quite staggered that customer service's first reaction was to assume I was a shoplifter.

"Oh, OK," he mumbled, taking my receipt. "We get quite a few homeless people coming in here trying to get cash for stuff they've just picked up off the shelves."

OK… so now he's suggesting I look homeless. Keep calm…

Finally, after being cheerily waved off with a scowl, I stepped back out into the foyer, quietly steaming with rage, only to hear, "Hello! Do you want to have a go?"

"Yes I do. I really do," I shouted at the happy rosy-cheeked face staring blankly back at me. A mother hastily guided her son past the nutter arguing with the aeroplane. I realised that I was now at one with the supermarket. I'd become so confrontational, I was picking fights with a kiddies' ride.

FANCY THAT!

Disastrous facts to make you go "wow"

More salt is used to clear roads of snow and ice than eaten.

A sneeze travels about 100 miles per hour.

In New York, it is illegal to sell a haunted house without telling the buyer.

Celery has negative calories. It takes more calories to eat a piece of celery than the celery has in it to begin with.

About 150 people per year are killed by coconuts.

Cherophobia is the fear of fun.

125,000 people injure themselves in bed each year.

During your lifetime, you will produce enough saliva to fill two swimming pools.

The chance of you dying on the way to get lottery tickets is actually greater than your chance of winning.

Women have twice as many pain receptors on their body than men. But a much higher pain tolerance.

Avocados are poisonous to birds.

Blue-eyed people tend to have the highest tolerance of alcohol.

Men are 6 times more likely to be struck by lightning than women.

The ancient Romans used to make a toothpaste that contained urine.

Skunks can accurately spray their smelly fluid as far as ten feet.

In 10 minutes, a hurricane releases more energy than all the world's nuclear weapons combined.

It's possible to lead a cow upstairs, but not downstairs.

There are more chickens than people in the world.

The average person spends 6 months of their lifetime waiting for a red light to turn green.

PICTURES: ISTOCKPHOTO, SHUTTERSTOCK

Chris Pascoe's Fun Tales

FLOOD FRACAS

Chris is definitely not getting along with water this week… or is he…?

I magine what it would be like living on a planet where there's a substance, present almost everywhere, which, depending on its state, can burn your skin off, suffocate you in minutes or freeze you to death – and, when particularly volatile, has enough power to completely destroy entire cities.

Well, that planet is Earth, the substance is water, and I live here. Typical.

That's a great little piece of trivia though, isn't it?

I mention it because water has played quite a large part in my life this week. Not that I hate water. I actually quite like it. Without it, beer wouldn't be possible. Rather less importantly, it keeps us all alive.

I still don't forgive it for this week though.

It all started, as most things in my life do, with a cat-sitting visit to another of my furry little friends – this one residing in a near mansion of a house whose kitchen had more floor space than my entire house and garden combined.

The only problem was that on this particular visit, much like my garden, it was covered in murky water and debris. It's testament to how wide awake I was that morning that I sloshed three feet into the room before even noticing I was ankle deep in water and the ceiling had fallen down.

I'd actually walked into a flooded house once before,

108

quite recently in fact, so I knew exactly what to do – and immediately did it. I ran round in circles with my hands on my head screaming "Oh no! Oh no!" That didn't seem to make much difference though, so next I rang Plumber Jim, who advised me to pull myself together, find the stopcock, and wait for his arrival.

OK I thought, stopcocks are often located in the cupboards under sinks. I quickly waded across the kitchen to the sink and dropped to my knees to look in the cupboard. I'll put it down to my state of panic that I dropped to my knees into a foot deep puddle of water, but I did, and when Jim arrived a few minutes later, he seemed more shocked by my dripping wet trousers than he did by the state of the kitchen.

I had sloshed into the room and not noticed it was flooded

A little while later, after Jim had found the actual location of the stopcock, turned the water off, and fixed the exploding toilet in the room above the kitchen, we sat with a nice cup of tea in the garden,

"Nice house, isn't it?" I remarked.

"Well, yeah, it was…"

With that, it was back to my reality – I was looking after a beautiful house that was now partially destroyed, but at least the cat was OK, and technically it was him I was caring for, not the upstairs toilet.

So now you know why I've got the hump with water this week. I absolutely hate the stuff right now.

Ah well, column written, time for a nice hot bath and then an ice cold beer.

Hmm, hang on… 🐾

CRASH COURSE!

A bike ride gets Chris up close and personal with more than just his relived youth

As I drive around on my weekend catsitting chores, I'm often struck by the sheer number of cyclists on the roads. Not your old style traditional cyclists on rickety black bikes, wearing hoopy shirts, berets and a string of onions draped round their necks… no wait, that's old style traditional Frenchmen, isn't it? Not them anyway, no. More your modern lycra-clad super-athletes, wearing trendy sun goggles and colourful aerodynamic go-faster helmets. They come out on Sundays in their hordes, sometimes in packs of at least 20, often four abreast across the road, leading me to sometimes wonder if I've taken a wrong turning and I'm driving round a velodrome.

Apart from doing their bit for society by ensuring I have no opportunity to ever break the speed limit – or even reach it – I have to admit that lately I've become a little bit jealous. Of all that fresh air, those thrilling descents down steep hills, the wind in their hair and the sun on their faces – all that stuff. So jealous in fact, that last weekend I fought my way to the back of our garage and dragged mine and Lorraine's mountain bikes into daylight for the first time in two decades.

Don't get me wrong, I wasn't about to attempt to spoon myself into anything lycra, mainly for fear of being arrested on public decency charges, but a ride through the local woods did seem like a good idea at the time.

And so it proved, for all of 90 seconds. That's how long it took us to reach our first hill, and as we walked along pushing our bikes, Lorraine grumbling about me and my bright ideas, I started to think we should've left the bikes where they belonged – in 1996.

Eventually though, we made it to the woods and things started improving as we took a gentle ride through beautiful woodland, the sun breaking through the treetops and squirrels darting across our paths. Then we reached the edge of a hill, and a breathtaking-downhill descent stretched away ahead of us. Lorraine went darting down the hill with me in close pursuit. Wonderful, exhilarating… until I hit a low-lying tree root at high speed. Suddenly, my bike vanished from beneath me, but I was still moving at 25 miles per hour. Lorraine glanced round to see what appeared to me running after her at breakneck speed, before disappearing over a ledge and crashing down face-first into a clump of stinging nettles.

"What do you think you're doing?" she shouted.

What do you think I'm doing? What do I think I'm doing? Competition sprinting followed by freestyle base-diving without

A breathtaking downhill descent stretched ahead of us

water? Had I not been lying face down with a mouth full of dirt, that's exactly what I'd have said. Instead it was more just, "Fnnnnarrggghhh," or words to that effect.

So, all in all a weekend in which I got reacquainted with some long lost loves. Firstly and obviously, my beloved old Townsend mountain bike, which is now on eBay, but also good old calamine lotion. Man, is that stuff good on nettle rash.

TEENAGE KICKS!

Only Chris could end up in the wrong when trying to agree with his daughter!

You will never win as a parent. Whether they're a toddler or a teen, the same rule applies – you're an idiot, they win and you lose. The only real difference is that when they're toddlers, they don't fully realise you lost so you sometimes get away with it.

This "no win" scenario was perfectly illustrated last weekend during a conversation with my now teenage daughter Maya, that I couldn't help but feel mirrored an exchange with the toddler Maya more than a decade earlier.

Our weekend conversation went like this: Maya walked into the kitchen and, with a huge grin on her face –slightly disturbing to see a teenager with a huge grin actually – told me about a forthcoming movie she'd just read about on the internet.

"OK Daddy, there's this guy right, who's bringing out his own movie, and it's going to be really, reallllly long."

"How long?"

"Well, put it this way, he's released a trailer that's over 7 hours long and next year he's doing a 72 hour trailer."

"What?" I replied, slightly stunned. "A three day trailer? How long's the movie?"

"720 hours! And it's only going to have one showing ever, and you can't record it so you'd have to watch it all in one go, but it's 30 days long so nobody would ever be able to watch it."

As she finished she gave a little shrug and shook her head incredulously. I couldn't help but agree with her sentiments, for once.

"That's stupid, isn't it!" I laughed. "Why the hell would anybody do all that, and then make it impossible to watch? That's just plain crazy!"

My reply was met with a stony silence. Maya's face dropped. What exactly had I missed here?

"Daddy, don't you think you're being extremely negative and shallow? If all you can do is make negative comments like that, I won't bother telling you anything."

With that, she turned on her heels and huffed out of the room. She wouldn't speak to me for three hours. I'd somehow agreed with everything I thought she'd said, and was still deemed to be totally wrong!

The incident that took place more than a decade earlier happened at The Goat Centre, that thrill-seekers' pleasure-centre of farmyard wonders often mentioned in earlier columns…

Sitting in the Happy Goat Café for lunch, I was, for reasons I won't go into, in a particularly downcast mood (I was often in a downcast mood at the Goat Centre).

An oblivious three-year-old Maya was happily playing her usual games, holding a big cup of milk to my face and repeating, "Hello, I'm a cup," over and over until I finally cracked and smiled at her.

Delighted, she shouted, "Speak to the cup, Daddy, speak to the cup."

"No, play with Mummy Maya, I'm not…"

"Speak to the cup, Daddy, speak to the cup."

"No Maya, I'm…"

"Speak to the cup, speak to the cup."

I sighed and gave in.

"Hello cup," I said.

"Don't you talk to me!" said the cup.

You see what I mean? 🐾

ALL AT SEA!

Chris gets in a spin on a raft and ends up baring all to the press…

Many years ago, I took part in an extravaganza on the River Thames called the Marlow Raft Race. Looking back, I now believe that never in the history of raft-racing – is there a history of raft racing? – could any crew have been less prepared than we were.

The team, formed in a pub, had been carefully selected, taking into account our existing and possible transferable skills…

Pub Landlord: "OK, listen up. We're entering a raft race. Anybody want to take part?"

All five semi-drunk people at the bar: "Me!"

So it was that four very unfit young gents with no sailing skills whatsoever, and one young lady who swore she didn't even remember volunteering, took to the Thames on a few wooden planks strapped to oil drums.

As the race began, we encountered our first serious problem.

I thought it was rather funny – until I was hit by a tomato!

A complete lack of research had led us to believe that the race was a race, and not a fight. Consequently, we were a little surprised when a barrage of eggs and tomatoes slammed into us from every neighbouring raft.

I remember the lad to my left hysterically screaming, "We're unarmed! We're supposed to be armed!" just before taking a fistful

splat!

splat!

BRITISH

of cold porridge to the face. I also recall finding this very funny – until I was hit by a tomato two seconds later.

One of our crew members bravely jumped ship and swam away. Then there were four. Our only recourse was to start paddling up-river as fast as we could, to get out of this huge free-for-all.

This we did and the barrage stopped, but not because we'd actually gone anywhere. Everybody else had proceeded up-river, but we were going round in circles. As we tried to ignore the laughing crowds on the riverbank and watched the raft flotilla disappear, one of our crew finally took decisive action – he reached into his rucksack and began munching on a sandwich.

Try as we might over the next half hour, we were unable to progress more than 10 yards forward. At one point we hit the riverbank and our female team mate took the opportunity to jump onto the grass and walk away.

Now there were three. Then, on the horizon, appeared the other rafts...they were coming back. The start line was also the finish line. Desperately we began trying to paddle the 10 yards back to the line, but all we did was complete another circle. We'd had it.

The last thing I remember before falling into the river was a raft-full of men in full protective clothing pulling alongside us, cheerily waving hello – and then completely covering us in manure.

The smell was incredible.

I stood, wavered, and then I was gone. As I tried to haul myself back onto the raft, I realised my shorts were riding rapidly downwards and I ended up mooning the entire crowd.

The only photos of me ever to appear in our local newspaper are one of me reading a children's book to an empty pile of beanbags... and one of my bare backside.

That's proof of how newsworthy I am...

DUTCH COURAGE!

Chris hoped a romantic trip to Amsterdam would have his partner going head over heels for him, but it seemed it was the other way round!

Although many would dispute it, I'm probably not the Missing Link between man and apes. But I'm pretty sure I'm the link between man and cats. Between two of them anyway – my dad and my old cat Brum.

As mentioned last week, the two had an uncanny amount in common, including an ability to knock themselves out and create fire and water disasters. The thing is, I'm no different and although I obviously had this handed down to me from my father like a poisoned chalice, the only explanation I can offer for Brum's ways is that he learned them from me.

After reading last week's column, my wife Lorraine was quick to point out a few "incidents" in our very early days together that strongly confirm the above.

After meeting me on the dance floor at a party where, due to my dance moves, we both ended up flat on the floor, she was then silly enough only months later to agree to join me on a weekend break in Amsterdam.

Never has one man done more in one weekend to convince a woman she'd be far better off single.

It all started in a very warm hotel bar, when I attempted to open a small fanlight window above our heads, totally failing to note

121

a thick iron bar loosely propped against it.

Lorraine didn't see the bar pitch forward and whack me full blast in the forehead. All she saw was me suddenly fall backwards past her chair as if in a dead faint, swiftly followed by an iron bar that smashed her wine glass into a thousand pieces.

It should've been hard to follow this, but I managed. Touring Amsterdam on hired rickety old push-bikes the following day, I realised within seconds that I was cycling on the wrong side of the road and heading straight for an on oncoming car. Grabbing for my brakes I discovered there weren't any.

Little did I know that old Dutch push-bikes typically have brakes attached to their pedals, and to stop you need to pedal backwards, rather than what I did, which was to throw my legs out to either side and shout, "Arghhhh!"

Not surprisingly, this didn't help much, and I rode straight into the car, whose driver had had the forethought to pull to a dead halt. I ended up sitting on its bonnet while my bike careered off into a wall.

As if this wasn't enough, while a now wary Lorraine consoled me 10 minutes later, I shakily propped my bike against a bin and leaned back on it in an attempt to regain some measure of composure. The bin, bike and, ultimately me, keeled over backwards and I ended up in a pile of rubbish with my legs up in the air. This was not an impressive look.

Little did I know that Dutch bikes have brakes attached to their pedals

I'm still completely amazed – and very grateful – she married me. All I can assume is that there was a certain style to my mishaps and, as everyone knows, falling with style is the next best thing to flying… 🐾

FOOTBALL CRAZY!

Pele, Beckham... Pascoe? No, Chris's name never made it up there with all the legends of the game – for very good reason

Back in my school days, I was surprisingly good at sport, generally reaching a standard just below mediocre. The most surprising thing of all though, was that in my final year at secondary school, I was picked for the school football team. Even the football coach was surprised by his own decision to pick me, seeing absolutely no skill in my play whatsoever.

However, against his better judgement he did so on the recommendations of his team captain and vice-captain, who just happened to be my two best friends.

So it was that I pulled on our school's coveted blue jersey for the first time on a rainy autumn day. This was another surprise, because I'd always been convinced we played in yellow, but it mattered not as the referee blew his whistle and our captain passed the ball straight to me. What happened next had our coach staring in astonishment.

As the ball reached my feet I looked at it for a second and realised I had no idea what to do with it, so I began running forwards. Luckily the ball came with me. As I kept running, in a state of blind panic, I realised my 'direct' approach had caught the opposition off guard and I was nearing their penalty area.

Only one thing to do; I kicked the ball as hard as I could towards the goal. I remember seeing it shooting off on completely the

wrong direction – but unbeknown to me, to one of our advancing players who immediately hammered it back into my path. By now I had absolutely no idea where the ball had gone… until it smacked me in the shins and rocketed straight into the roof of the goal. To the bewilderment of everyone around me, I'd scored 20 seconds into my debut… by accident.

The wonderful thing was, I was the only one who actually knew it was an accident. I'm told the football coach actually dropped his clipboard in surprise and his jaw fell open. He probably believed he'd discovered a school-park Pele.

What happened next had our coach staring in astonishment

And that was it. I never scored another goal. My only other claim to fame was being substituted during the last game of the season for tactical reasons (being rubbish), then being asked by the referee to assist him as a stand-in linesman… and then getting sent off by the same referee five minutes later, possibly the only linesman to be sent off in the history of football. So I did achieve something. Not something good of course, but I achieved it!

After leaving school, I persisted in the beautiful game, much against people's advice, and my play became very consistent, in that I consistently scored own-goals. So many own-goals in fact, that my goalkeeper voted for me in the end of season awards, as his 'Most Difficult Opponent.'

So there you have it, a few reasons why my friends are wrong to claim my football career was a disaster. It was much worse than that.

IN FOR A SHOCK!

Chris can't work out how to close a window and wrecks the place...

Never mess with things you know nothing about. I've been guilty of ignoring that sound advice this week while trying my best to demolish a house. The house wasn't actually up for demolition, and customers generally don't like their catsitter to provide this service, so it's just as well I failed. Partially failed, anyway.

From the moment I arrived, things started to go wrong. Firstly, the cat was wrong – as in the cat that greeted me wasn't the cat I was supposed to be looking after, but rather some big tabby chancer who'd climbed in through the bathroom window. After the tabby made his apologies and left, I set about attempting to close the offending window.

I couldn't. Well, not this window anyway. It was one of those clever multiple-setting windows that open in three different directions, something I only realised upon giving it a good hard tug to check it was now secure. The completely un-shut window flew open, knocking a vase of flowers off the windowsill which shattered on the floor and sending me sprawling backwards into the bathtub. My arms flailed to grab a shower curtain, so I went into the tub, rail and all.

Great start, I thought as I clambered out of the bath, but decided I'd have to deal with the damage later – a cat needed feeding and was shouting to tell me so from the kitchen.

As I watched Jasper the Ginger eat, a strange item on the kitchen worktop caught my eye. It looked like a toy tennis racquet, but its strings were at three different overset levels and there was a small button and light on the handle. Picking it up, I stood and pondered it for quite some time.

I decided it clearly was a toy tennis racquet, and reasoned that pressing the button might simulate the noise of a tennis ball hitting the strings. I pressed the button and took a swipe…nothing. The little red light illuminated but there was no sound at all. Maybe it has to connect with something, I thought. Pressing the button again, I slapped the racquet gently against the palm of my left hand…

My shock at the outcome was off the scale. I received a huge electric shock to my hand, causing me to throw my arm involuntarily backwards, sending a teapot crashing to the floor.

What on earth just happened? Unusually for me, I didn't try to work it out by having another go – my left hand was stinging far too much for that. Also, I didn't actually need to because I'd just spotted, far too late, some tiny words on the base of the racquet's handle. It seems I'd just smacked myself with an electronic mosquito swatter.

The window flew open sending me sprawling into the bath

As my daughter Maya so eloquently put it later that day, "Why would anybody do something like that? You complete idiot!"

Yes, idiot indeed. I'd been in a customer's house barely five minutes and had not only wrecked the bathroom and kitchen but almost electrocuted myself to boot!

It's a very good job I'm insured, really… 🐾

REG THE BUILDER

A retired tradesman becomes Chris's new best friend – and kindred spirit

We recently engaged the services of a 78-year-old retired builder called Reg to fix our leaking roof. He told us it would take a day or two but he spent so long with us, he became a close family friend.

Funnily enough, and unbeknown to us for the first seven weeks of his two-day job, he'd actually lived next door to my Mum during the Second World War.

I saw Reg's ad in a local magazine and, as we'd been trying to get a builder, any builder, to come and look at our roof for three months, I liked the sound of his "no job too small" banner-line.

When he turned up to give us an estimate, it was actually a heart attack he almost gave us. A 78-year-old clambering onto your roof from a precariously thin and unstable wall over a 20- foot drop, chatting happily as pieces of masonry crashed to the ground, is enough to set anybody's heart racing.

The estimate was good however, as was his resolve to fix the wall he'd just broken, so we immediately said yes. We had to, really. We'd had an indoor water feature every time it rained.

The next day, Reg called us and said he planned to make a start that morning. Then he called again to ask us to remind him where we lived. We were going to be out until lunchtime, but Reg said he could start without us.

This was probably a mistake, because we arrived home to find

him on next door's roof removing tiles.

Reg watched us arrive at our front door from his rooftop perch and after a brief silence, realised his error and shouted that he'd better just quickly repair next door's roof, he'd be straight over. We next saw him two weeks later.

This time he made some real progress, managing to fix the leak but diverting rain straight through our letterbox.

We arrived home to find him on next door's roof removing tiles

Over the ensuing weeks, and hundreds of cups of tea, I got to know Reg very well. He had some great stories to tell, and was one of the most likeable chaps I think I'll ever meet. The fact that one story involved him explaining how he'd made it through 50 years in the building industry without ever fully knowing what he was doing didn't fill me with confidence, but he was still great to chat to!

When Reg finally finished his work, we shook hands and didn't see him again for two months. Which was odd, because half his tools were still in our garden. We finally thought we'd better call and ask if he'd like to retrieve them, and spoke to his wife.

"Oh, that's great, he'll be straight round!" she exclaimed. "He's been wondering what happened to them!"

Ten days on we still have the tools, but I'm hopeful he'll be back. I'm keeping the teapot warm.

CALAMITY JAMES!

At last, someone other than Chris will be the butt of the pub jokes…

There's a friend of mine named Jim who reads my column in My Weekly and then tells everybody in our local pub exactly what I've been up to.

"You'll never guess what he did last week. Damn near electrocuted himself! The man's a liability!"

Consequently, every time I walk into that pub, I spend the first five minutes facing down a barrage of amused mickey-taking. I do get sympathy pints though, so I don't mind at all.

What I do mind is that Jim is a good, sensible kind of guy and never does anything ridiculous or daft, so I rarely have any sort of come-back to offer at all.

Until now.

To my surprise, when I walked into the pub last night, I received the usual vocal barrage, but with one major difference – nobody could wait to tell me exactly what Jim had been up to.

The pub had hosted their yearly Christmas charity pool tournament the weekend before, and Jim chose this event to propel himself from straight-man Jim to Calamity James and into the pages of My Weekly.

Jim started the evening well enough, looking the part in his elf onesie and winning his first pool match with ease. It was then his troubles began. Lining up his cue to take a shot in his second round match, he somehow pulled it back way too hard, lost grip,

and propelled it straight through the air into the pub Christmas tree.

Not content with this, he then made a desperate lunge to retrieve it, accidentally swinging it wildly enough to send baubles flying in all directions before raising his now tinsel-covered cue sharply up to a sudden halt.

Unfortunately, the thing that had brought the cue to a halt was the referee – and a very sensitive part of the referee at that. Most people thought the ref a bit harsh to disqualify Jim, but given he was crying at the time, his judgment was clouded.

That would probably have been enough, but Jim wasn't finished.

A little later, and possibly after a mulled wine or two, Jim was settling on his bar stool to watch the last few shots of the tournament final when his backside slipped off the stool and he found himself pitching forward towards the floor. In a desperate attempt to prevent the inevitable, he began running in a high speed crouching-waddle straight at the pool table.

Jim looked the part in his elf onesie as he won the pool game

The fact he was able to stop himself hitting the floor was quite an achievement, but as he did it by slamming headlong into the pool table… it probably wasn't.

As he clambered up the side of the table, the left lens of his specs shattered in comedy fashion and he inadvertently swept his hand across the pool table baize, thus completely disrupting the final.

The fact that Jim actually asked me to write his story here suggests to me that he may not have fully recovered from his knock on the head.

It'll be fun when he reads this one out, though! 🐾

INSULT AND INJURY

A case of tennis elbow causes a whole host of festive catastrophes

I've just had the week from hell. Over the course of the last few days, while trying to prepare for Christmas, I somehow acquired tennis elbow even though I've never played tennis in my life. The tennis elbow has caused total havoc, but I also managed to get a thorn embedded in my head, and to cap it all, looked like a total madman in public – again.

OK, firstly the tennis elbow. Apparently you don't need to be Andy Murray to develop this condition, just push doors too hard. I have a habit of over-checking I've shut front doors, sometimes to the point of destruction, and the repetitive strain eventually took its toll on my right elbow.

Tennis elbow is a funny condition – it feels a bit achy, but I also get sudden muscle spasms, causing me to fling my right arm out in random directions.

It's created havoc with my Christmas decorating. Never has a Christmas tree been punched so hard and so often, much to the amusement of Bodmin, my ever-watching cat. One moment I'd be carefully hanging a bauble, the next violently throwing the bauble into the air for Bodmin to hunt down and kill.

But, it was the moment my toddler niece proudly handed me a meticulously handcrafted string of paper chains that I was finally relieved of decorating duties. After thanking little Chloe for her wonderful gift, she'd no sooner turned her back when, to her

mother's stunned disbelief, I suddenly ripped the paper chain in half and hurled it to the floor, with what appeared to be a look of fury on my face (it was actually pain).

So, banished to the garden to stick a few 'SANTA STOP HERE' signs in the ground, I found myself crouching just below a particularly spiky branch. After driving Santa into the grass, I stood up far too sharply and connected with the branch. Rubbing my head and cursing, I realised with alarm that there was something sticking out of it. I rushed back into the house, bravely screaming for help. I can't tell you how impressed Lorraine looked when, in front of everyone, I explained that I'd got a thorn stuck in my head. I'd only been gone three minutes.

Lorraine tried in vain to remove it but her efforts only caused it to sink further in. Finally, all that remained visible was a small black dot.

It was down to A&E for me, where a slightly amused nurse plastered my head in magnesium sulphate to draw the thorn out and stuck a plaster over it, more to my hair than my head, telling me to come back the following day.

Never has a Christmas tree been punched so hard and so often

On my way out, I decided to cheer myself up with a mince pie from the hospital canteen. I stepped outside into the warm winter sunshine and took a bite. It was delicious. Suddenly life seemed a whole lot better.

Smiling happily, I suddenly winced, my elbow spasmed, and with a flick of my wrist I threw the entire contents of my pie-case onto the pavement…

My Weekly Pocket Novels

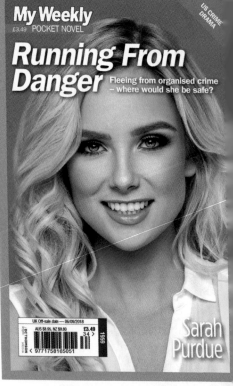

For women who love great stories

◆ Handy handbag size

◆ Full of drama and romance

My Weekly Specials

Great fiction, mind-stretching puzzles, health and wellbeing

5 EXCLUSIVE STORIES FROM TOP AUTHORS + 50 BOOKS to win!

Aug 21 – Aug 28, 2018
No 5438

No 1 For Fiction

£1.20

My Weekly

www.myweekly.co.uk

BEST EVER Chocolate Cake!

STEP-BY-STEP

THE MAGIC OF LAPLAND

10 WAYS TO BEAT ANXIETY

SAVE OVER 17%
12 ISSUES FOR ONLY £12

AND LOVING IT!

My Weekly magazine brings you the perfect mix of great reading to inspire and entertain. We're No 1 for fiction, with entertaining short stories and serials from best-selling authors and up-and-coming writers.

It's easy to order!

FREEPHONE: **0800 318 846** quoting **MWEM**

(Free from UK landlines and mobiles only) 8am-6pm Mon-Fri, 9am-5pm Sat. Overseas: +44 1382 5755

BY POST send coupon overleaf to:

My Weekly Subscriptions, PO Box 766, Haywards Heath, RH16 9G

For one-off payment orders, enclose your details and a cheque made payable to DC Thomson & Co Ltd

UNMISSABLE TRIAL OFFER! £8
Your favourite reads from only £8

SAVE OVER 33%
3 ISSUES FOR ONLY £8

SAVE OVER 62%
6 ISSUES FOR ONLY £8

The Specials are packed full with all the exciting stories and features that our readers enjoy! There will be interviews with your favourite celebrities, real life stories, fun puzzles, up-to-date fashion and beauty news, and great cookery for you to try.

My Weekly Pocket Novels make an essential component of life for anyone who enjoys reading fiction, love, romance and thrillers. Each issue will leave you feeling like you've been on an emotional rollercoaster ride.

ONLINE: **www.myweekly.co.uk/emtrial**

ORDER FORM

Please complete the coupon below and send it to: My Weekly Subscriptions, DC Thomson Shop, PO Box 766, Haywards Heath, RH16 9GF

YES, I would like a trial subscription to (tick all that apply):

❑ **My Weekly** - 12 issues for only £12 (UK) or £20 (overseas)

❑ **My Weekly Special** - 3 issues for only £8 (UK) or £11 (overseas)

❑ **My Weekly Pocket Nove**l - 6 issues for only £8 (UK) or £16 (overseas)

Your Details

Title .... Name.. Address ....

....Postcode ....

Telephone...Email ....

Delivery Details (If different from above)

Title .... Name...Address ....

....Postcode ....

Telephone...

DIRECT DEBIT

DIRECT Debit

INSTRUCTIONS TO YOUR BANK/BUILDING SOCIETY TO PAY BY DIRECT DEBIT

Originator's Identification Number

3	8	8	5	5	2

Name and full postal address of your Bank or Building Society

To the Manager	Bank/Building Society
Address	
	Postcode

Instruction to your Bank or Building Society
Please pay DC Thomson & Co Ltd Direct debit from the account detailed in this instruction subject to the safeguards assured by the Direct Debit Guarantee. I understand that this instruction may remain with DC Thomson & Co Ltd and if so, details will be passed electronically to my Bank/Building society.

Signature(s)

Name(s) of A/c Holder(s)

Date

Bank/Building Account No

FOR DC THOMSON & CO LTD OFFICIAL USE ONLY
This is not part of the instruction to your Bank or Building society.

Branch Sort Code

Bank and Building Societies may not accept Direct Debits for some types of account

DC Thomson & Co. Ltd and its group companies would like to contact you about new products, services and offers we think may be of interest to you. If you'd like to hear from us by post, please tick here ❑ telephone, please tick here • or email, please tick here ❑ From time to time, carefully chosen partner businesses would like to contact you with relevant offers. If you'd like to hear from partner businesses for this purpose please tick here ❑